W9-BCK-633

Capital Punishment

Other Books in the Current Controversies Series:

The Abortion Controversy
Alcoholism
Assisted Suicide
Computers and Society
Conserving the Environment
Crime
The Disabled
Drug Trafficking
Ethics
Europe
Family Violence
Free Speech
Gambling
Garbage and Waste
Gay Rights
Genetics and Intelligence
Gun Control
Guns and Violence
Hate Crimes
Hunger
Illegal Drugs
Illegal Immigration
The Information Highway
Interventionism
Iraq
Marriage and Divorce
Medical Ethics
Mental Health
Minorities
Nationalism and Ethnic Conflict
Native American Rights
Police Brutality
Politicians and Ethics
Pollution
Prisons
Racism
Reproductive Technologies
The Rights of Animals
Sexual Harassment
Smoking
Teen Addiction
Urban Terrorism
Violence Against Women
Violence in the Media
Women in the Military

Capital Punishment

Mary E. Williams, *Book Editor*

David Bender, *Publisher*
Bruno Leone, *Executive Editor*

Bonnie Szumski, *Editorial Director*
David M. Haugen, *Managing Editor*

CURRENT CONTROVERSIES

Cover photo: ©1998 Thor Swift/Impact Visuals

Library of Congress Cataloging-in-Publication Data

Capital punishment / Mary E. Williams, book editor.
p. cm. — (Current controversies)
Includes bibliographical references and index.
ISBN 0-7377-0141-2 (lib. : alk. paper). — ISBN 0-7377-0140-4 (pbk. : alk. paper)
1. Capital punishment—United States. 2. Capital punishment—Moral and ethical aspects—United States. 3. Discrimination in capital punishment—United States. I. Williams, Mary E., 1960– . II. Series.
HV8699.U5C2923 2000
364.66'0973—dc21 99-40319
CIP

Printed in the U.S.A.

Contents

Chapter 4: Should Capital Punishment Be Abolished?

Foreword

By definition, controversies are "discussions of questions in which opposing opinions clash" (Webster's Twentieth Century Dictionary Unabridged). Few would deny that controversies are a pervasive part of the human condition and exist on virtually every level of human enterprise. Controversies transpire between individuals and among groups, within nations and between nations. Controversies supply the grist necessary for progress by providing challenges and challengers to the status quo. They also create atmospheres where strife and warfare can flourish. A world without controversies would be a peaceful world; but it also would be, by and large, static and prosaic.

The Series' Purpose

The purpose of the Current Controversies series is to explore many of the social, political, and economic controversies dominating the national and international scenes today. Titles selected for inclusion in the series are highly focused and specific. For example, from the larger category of criminal justice, Current Controversies deals with specific topics such as police brutality, gun control, white collar crime, and others. The debates in Current Controversies also are presented in a useful, timeless fashion. Articles and book excerpts included in each title are selected if they contribute valuable, long-range ideas to the overall debate. And wherever possible, current information is enhanced with historical documents and other relevant materials. Thus, while individual titles are current in focus, every effort is made to ensure that they will not become quickly outdated. Books in the Current Controversies series will remain important resources for librarians, teachers, and students for many years.

In addition to keeping the titles focused and specific, great care is taken in the editorial format of each book in the series. Book introductions and chapter prefaces are offered to provide background material for readers. Chapters are organized around several key questions that are answered with diverse opinions representing all points on the political spectrum. Materials in each chapter include opinions in which authors clearly disagree as well as alternative opinions in which authors may agree on a broader issue but disagree on the possible solutions. In this way, the content of each volume in Current Controversies mirrors the mosaic of opinions encountered in society. Readers will quickly realize that there are many viable answers to these complex issues. By questioning each author's conclusions, students and casual readers can begin to develop the critical thinking skills so important to evaluating opinionated material.

Current Controversies is also ideal for controlled research. Each anthology in the series is composed of primary sources taken from a wide gamut of informational categories including periodicals, newspapers, books, United States and foreign government documents, and the publications of private and public organizations. Readers will find factual support for reports, debates, and research papers covering all areas of important issues. In addition, an annotated table of contents, an index, a book and periodical bibliography, and a list of organizations to contact are included in each book to expedite further research.

Perhaps more than ever before in history, people are confronted with diverse and contradictory information. During the Persian Gulf War, for example, the public was not only treated to minute-to-minute coverage of the war, it was also inundated with critiques of the coverage and countless analyses of the factors motivating U.S. involvement. Being able to sort through the plethora of opinions accompanying today's major issues, and to draw one's own conclusions, can be a complicated and frustrating struggle. It is the editors' hope that Current Controversies will help readers with this struggle.

Greenhaven Press anthologies primarily consist of previously published material taken from a variety of sources, including periodicals, books, scholarly journals, newspapers, government documents, and position papers from private and public organizations. These original sources are often edited for length and to ensure their accessibility for a young adult audience. The anthology editors also change the original titles of these works in order to clearly present the main thesis of each viewpoint and to explicitly indicate the opinion presented in the viewpoint. These alterations are made in consideration of both the reading and comprehension levels of a young adult audience. Every effort is made to ensure that Greenhaven Press accurately reflects the original intent of the authors included in this anthology.

"Although public support for capital punishment remains strong, concern about the possibility of wrongful executions is reflected in the writings of criminologists, lawmakers, and theologians."

Introduction

In the spring of 1993, Morris Gauger and his wife, Ruth Gauger, were bludgeoned and stabbed to death on their family farm near Richmond, Illinois. Their son, forty-year-old Gary Gauger, phoned 911 after he and a friend discovered his father's body on the floor of the antique motorcycle shop located at the farm. Police became suspicious when they arrived to find an oddly serene Gary Gauger, who calmly tended to his vegetable garden during the investigators' search for evidence. After discovering the body of Ruth Gauger—but no signs of struggle or attempted robbery—police subjected Gauger to twenty-one hours of intensive questioning. During this interrogation, Gauger later reported, detectives claimed that they had a "stack of evidence" proving that he had committed the murders. It did not occur to Gauger that his accusers might be lying.

Gauger, a pot smoker and reformed alcoholic at the time of the murders, became convinced that he had blacked out—as he did on occasion when he was a heavy drinker—and killed his parents. The interrogators, reportedly trying to jog Gauger's memory, showed him photos of his mother's wounds and asked him to hypothetically recreate the murders. Gauger described how he might have easily sneaked up behind his "trusting" mother before striking her head and slashing her throat, and then doing the same to his father. The police accepted Gauger's statements as a confession. After his trial in October 1993, a jury took three hours to reach a guilty verdict. Judge Henry Cowling sentenced Gauger to death by lethal injection.

Soon after Gauger's conviction, FBI agents reported that they had overheard members of a motorcycle club discussing questionable details about the Gauger murders. Ginger Gauger, Gary's sister, then enlisted Northwestern University Law School professor Lawrence Marshall to help with her brother's appeal. Marshall was able to prove that there was no real evidence against Gauger and that he had been tricked into giving a false confession. Eventually, two motorcyclists were indicted for the murders of Ruth and Morris Gauger, and Gary Gauger's sentence and conviction were overturned.

Gary Gauger's case may be astonishing, but it is not unusual. Since the United States Supreme Court reinstated the death penalty in 1976, at least five hundred people have been executed. Between 1976 and 1999, seventy-five death-row inmates have been released after new information revealed that they had been wrongfully convicted. Thus, for every seven executions, one condemned inmate has been exonerated. "If you had to go to a hospital for a life-and-death operation and found that the hospital misdiagnosed [one out of seven] cases, you'd run," commented lawyer Barry Scheck, one of the speakers at a 1998 conference on wrongful death-penalty convictions held at Northwestern University Law School. "It's an intolerable level of error, regardless of your views on the death penalty."

Americans' overwhelming support of capital punishment, death penalty critics maintain, is based on the assumption that only people who are guilty of premeditated murder are being executed. However, for various reasons, innocent people can end up on death row. Faulty eyewitness identifications, false testimony—often presented by "jailhouse snitches" seeking to get reduced sentences, badly handled evidence, and inept legal representation can lead to wrongful convictions. In Gary Gauger's case, police elicited a false confession by being deceptive during interrogation. Such investigative trickery is legal because it may help to capture wily criminals. But an innocent person who trusts the police can end up as the accused in a murder case. "My parents had just been murdered and [the police] were the good guys," says Gauger. "I know it sounds naïve now, but when they told me they wouldn't lie to me, I believed them."

According to death penalty opponents, the wrongly convicted are often "outsiders": racial minorities, people with mild mental retardation, the mentally ill, or nonconformists. During Gauger's murder trial, for example, prosecutors painted Gauger as a drug-using eccentric and ex-commune dweller who could have easily "turned" on his parents. The death penalty has often been denounced for being unfairly applied to minorities; compounding this problem, critics point out, are the recently imposed restrictions on the death-penalty appeals process. In an effort to keep condemned prisoners from using repeated appeals simply to postpone their executions, Congress passed the 1996 Anti-Terrorism and Effective Death Penalty Act, which limits convicts to one appeal in most cases. Some legal experts maintain that the law increases the chances that innocent people will be executed because it reduces opportunities for exonerating evidence to arise. In 1997, partly in response to the 1996 congressional legislation, the American Bar Association called for a voluntary moratorium on executions "unless and until greater fairness and due process prevail in death penalty implementation." Opponents of capital punishment, furthermore, contend that the unfair and arbitrary manner in which the death penalty is administered warrants its abolition.

Supporters of the death penalty, on the other hand, are often skeptical about the innocence of death-row inmates whose convictions have been overturned. They are concerned that exonerations of the "wrongly convicted" may be based on irrelevant legal technicalities rather than solid evidence that proves innocence. In response to the 1998 colloquium on the wrongly convicted held at Northwestern University Law School, Diane Clements, president of the victims' rights group Justice for All, stated that "of the seventy-five exonerated prisoners that they highlighted at the conference, even the conference organizers said they could not prove innocence. Along with everybody else in the United States, Justice for All does not want to see innocents wrongly convicted. But were these people really innocent?"

Other defenders of capital punishment maintain that today's improved investigative techniques, such as DNA testing, are making it less likely that people will be wrongly executed. For instance, former death-row inmates Dennis Williams and Verneal Jimerson, who had both been convicted of the 1978 murder of an Illinois couple, were exonerated after recent DNA tests revealed that neither could have been involved in the crime. Some death penalty advocates argue that the case of Williams and Jimerson and other similar exonerations indicate that the criminal justice system actually works quite effectively. Moreover, these advocates contend, sentences for murder err toward leniency rather than the other way around. Susan Smith, for example, who was convicted of drowning her two children in 1994, was sentenced to life in prison. "Unabomber" Theodore Kaczynski, who had mailed letter bombs that killed three and injured twenty-two, was also sentenced to life in prison. Murderers' lives are usually spared when there is a possibility that they are mentally incompetent, death penalty supporters point out.

Many capital punishment advocates believe, furthermore, that the possibility of executing the innocent does not justify the abolition of the death penalty. Even if a few innocent lives are taken, they argue, the deterrent effects of the death penalty are worth it. As Detroit lawyer Stephen Markman puts it, "the death penalty serves to protect a vastly greater number of innocent lives than are likely to be lost through its erroneous application . . . a society would be guilty of a suicidal failure of nerve if it were to forgo the use of an appropriate and deserved punishment simply because it is not humanly possible to eliminate the risk of mistake entirely." Public opinion reflects Markman's contention: A June 1995 Gallup poll showed that 57 percent of Americans would still favor the death penalty even if one out of one hundred of those executed were undeniably innocent.

Although public support for capital punishment remains strong, concern about the possibility of wrongful executions is reflected in the writings of criminologists, lawmakers, and theologians. *Capital Punishment: Current Controversies* explores this topic as well as arguments concerning the ethics, fairness, and deterrent effects of the death penalty. Its various authors provide a compelling examination of the enduring issues surrounding the death sentence.

Chapter 1

Is Capital Punishment Ethical?

Chapter Preface

Most societies at some time or other have endorsed the use of the death penalty. Ancient Roman and Judaic cultures practiced retributive justice, adhering to the rule of "an eye for an eye." The United States inherited its use of capital punishment from European settlers in the seventeenth century, promoting the notion that heinous crimes deserved severe punishment. In the eighteenth century, however, philosophers began to question the ethics of the death penalty. Italian criminologist Cesare Beccaria condemned capital punishment as an ineffective and grossly inhumane deterrent to crime. Conversely, German philosopher Immanuel Kant claimed that execution was the fairest punishment for murder, arguing that even guilt-ridden killers should die in order to gain release from their anguish. Such arguments concerning the ethics of capital punishment continue to spark controversy to the present day.

Contemporary supporters of capital punishment maintain that execution is the most suitable penalty for those who have deliberately committed murder. They contend that the principles of modern criminal justice require a murderer to face a punishment that is comparable to the harm caused by his crime. Moreover, supporters argue, the death penalty enables society to uphold the worth of innocent human life and to express its justified moral outrage at the crime of murder. In the words of criminal justice author Robert James Bidinotto, "America was founded on the principle that each individual is an end in himself. In such a society, premeditated murder is a crime in a class by itself. Murder negates the highest moral end of civil society: the irreplaceable human life. What possible penalty could be proportionate to such a crime, except the forfeiture of the murderer's own life?"

Modern-day critics of capital punishment, on the other hand, contend that murder—whether committed by an individual or by the government—is morally wrong and can never be justified. For one thing, many argue, the mental anguish experienced by people who have been condemned to death is a form of torture, and the practice of torture has been denounced by the internationally supported Universal Declaration of Human Rights. Furthermore, death penalty opponents maintain, when the state executes killers in an attempt to proclaim that murder is wrong, it undermines its moral authority and ultimately denies the value of each human life. According to anti-death penalty activist Helen Prejean, "The death penalty *costs* too much. Allowing our [U.S.] government to kill citizens compromises the deepest moral values upon which this country was conceived: the inviolable dignity of human persons."

Included among the authors in the following chapter are criminologists and theologians who present several strongly opinionated arguments concerning the ethics of the death penalty.

Capital Punishment Is Moral

by Robert James Bidinotto

About the author: *Robert James Bidinotto is an award-winning journalist and the author of* Freed to Kill. *He is also the editor of* Criminal Justice? The Legal System Vs. Individual Responsibility.

On March 25, 1996, officials of the Florida Department of Corrections strapped condemned killer Pedro Medina into the electric chair at Florida State Prison. Like 38 other infamous murderers since 1976, including serial killer Ted Bundy, Medina would meet his end in the embrace of "Old Sparky."

This time, however, the 74-year-old oak electric chair more than lived up to its grisly name—and in the process, re-opened the age-old debate over the morality of the death penalty.

After the black leather mask was lowered over Medina's face, the first of three surges of 2,000 volts of electricity jolted his body. He lurched back in the chair. Suddenly flames shot up from the mask, and burned for perhaps ten seconds. The death chamber filled with smoke.

Death penalty opponents immediately cited the gruesome nature of the execution to call once again for an end to capital punishment.

"It was brutal, terrible," declared witness Michael Minerva. "It was a burning alive, literally." Minerva—a defense lawyer for a taxpayer-supported state agency that defends death row inmates—demanded that the governor halt all pending executions.

"When you torture someone to death," added Robyn Blumner, executive director of the Florida chapter of the American Civil Liberties Union, "the Eighth Amendment [barring "cruel and unusual" punishment] clearly has been violated."

Of course, Medina hadn't been "burned alive" or "tortured to death." The medical examiner later said that he'd found no signs that Medina had suffered or felt any prolonged pain; most likely, he had died almost instantly. But the truth hardly mattered; the charges of suffering and torture were only the latest

Reprinted, with permission, from "The *Moral* Case for Capital Punishment," by Robert James Bidinotto, *LEAA Advocate*, Summer/Fall 1997.

of many spurious arguments employed by death penalty opponents during Medina's long appeal process.

Medina himself had been the most cynical of the claimants. Not only did he maintain his innocence of the murder for which he was convicted; he also argued, on appeal, that he should not have been given the death penalty even if guilty. His reason: the trial court had erred in finding in his crime aggravating factors of "heinous, atrocious, or cruel and for pecuniary gain"—factors necessary for imposing a death-penalty sentence.

Meriting the Death Penalty

A review of the facts, however, suggests otherwise, and provides some telling insights concerning the morality of capital punishment.

You may recall that in 1980, Fidel Castro cleansed his nation of some 125,000 criminals, mentally ill, and other "undesirables" during the notorious "Mariel boatlift." Pedro Medina was among Castro's castoffs.

Once in America, Medina nurtured dreams of upward mobility, symbolized by having a car of his own. Appeals court records describe it as a "tremendous desire," even "an obsession." By 1982, Medina also had a jailed girlfriend, another source of frustration.

He gained the friendship and sympathy of Dorothy James, a 52-year-old mother and schoolteacher. And it turns out that Mrs. James had a car—just the kind of car Medina yearned for.

A simple, direct sort of man, Medina did the only practical thing: in order to obtain the car, he stabbed his "friend," Mrs. James, to death. He wasn't very skilled at it, but he was persistent. In fact, he inflicted a total of ten wounds—six to her chest, one in her neck, another in her abdomen, and two more to her left wrist. Even so, Dorothy James wouldn't die.

Irritated, Medina jammed a gag in her mouth. The medical examiner later determined that Mrs. James, in physical agony, took up to a half hour to die.

Pedro Medina finally had the car of his dreams. Unfortunately, in his excitement, he left his hat behind at the murder scene. Eventually, he decided that it actually might be better to sell the hot car, in order to raise bail for his girlfriend. But negotiations didn't go well with a prospective buyer. So, Medina stabbed and robbed that guy, too.

> ***"Capital punishment . . . is the only punishment roughly proportionate to the harm that has been done to the murder victim."***

Police caught up with Pedro Medina in Lake City, Florida. They found him asleep at the side of the road in Mrs. James' stolen car. At his trial, Medina was asked to try on the hat which had been recovered from the murder scene. It fit perfectly. Being a simple, direct sort of man, Medina then asked the judge if he could keep the hat. "You've got to be kidding!" the judge exclaimed.

He was convicted of murder and given the death penalty.

Years of appeals and endless protestations of innocence failed to sway a small army of appellate judges, who affirmed that his murder of Dorothy James had been "heinous, atrocious, or cruel and for pecuniary gain"—thus meriting the death penalty.

Addressing the Moral Claims of Death Penalty Opponents

Of course, that didn't persuade death penalty opponents that putting him to death was right and just. They argued, in effect, that however heinous and cruel, Medina's murder of Dorothy James should be irrelevant to the degree of punishment he might receive. He should not be punished in proportion to the harm he had caused an innocent woman; he should not get "revenge," or "just desserts," or "an eye for an eye"; he should not receive justice, but rather, mercy.

This argument, typical of death penalty opponents, is based on several unstated, and usually unchallenged, moral premises:

- that mercy is ethically superior to justice (which they call "revenge");
- that all human life—even that of a killer—has "intrinsic value," so that it's immoral to take another's life under any circumstances; and
- that society's response to a crime shouldn't be proportionate to the harm caused by the criminal, but governed by other considerations.

How do supporters of the death penalty answer such claims? Too often, they ignore or evade these moral questions at the core of the debate, and instead try to advance "practical" (or utilitarian) arguments for capital punishment.

For example, they typically base their case on the notion that capital punishment is a necessary measure for "crime control." From this, they go on to argue (a) that capital punishment incapacitates (or prevents) the killer from ever repeating his crime, and (b) that the existence of a death penalty deters future murders by frightening other would-be killers.

Now it's certainly true that executing a convicted killer will prevent him from ever committing another murder. It's also probably true that some unknown number of potential killers might hesitate, out of fear of being put to death themselves.

But there are two major problems with this line of argument. First, it begs the moral question: it doesn't address the moral claims of death penalty opponents.

Second, as primary objectives of the law, deterrence and incapacitation don't aim primarily to punish a past offense, but rather to prevent future ones. And that can lead to gross injustices.

Criminal Justice "Looks Backwards"

To elaborate on this second point: as a response to crime, punishment "looks backwards," into the past—to the criminal's specific past crimes and victims.

You punish someone for bad things he already did. By contrast, so-called crime-control measures "look forward," into the future, trying to reduce the rates of future crime. They don't directly address what someone already did; rather, they try indirectly to alter what he might do. They largely forget the criminal's past crimes—and his past victims.

But aren't the past victims of central importance to our system of justice? If preventing future crime is the main goal of the criminal law, then we could easily reduce the number of future murders by blindly imposing brutal penalties on all potential killers—penalties that most people would find to be grossly unfair and disproportionate.

For example, since most killers have escalated from less serious crimes, we might execute all those convicted of any violent crime. That way, we'd be sure to eliminate a significant number of budding killers, and reduce future murder rates. Or, since killers share many psychological characteristics, we might execute any criminal who fit a psychological profile that places them at high risk for future violence. In fact, if reducing the future crime rate were the only consideration in how we punish people, we could simply execute all criminals, from petty to serious. Surely that would be an effective crime control measure. But would anyone think it was fair or just? Should a pickpocket and a serial killer merit exactly the same punishment?

A "crime control" agenda based strictly on deterrence and incapacitation can also lead to unexpected leniency. That's because if reducing future murders is all that matters, then it's not logical or cost-effective to execute those murderers who are unlikely either to repeat their crimes, or to inspire "copycats."

> ***"Capital punishment for proven premeditated murders is . . . not immoral; it is not even a 'necessary evil'; it is a moral necessity, demanded by justice."***

For example, most people would probably agree that Susan Smith, the woman who drowned her own children, would be unlikely ever to repeat such an atrocity.

Nor would her unspeakable act be likely to encourage other mothers to drown their own babies, even if she went unpunished. Well, then why bother punishing her at all, let alone with a death penalty?

Solely on the "practical" grounds of deterrence or incapacitation, it doesn't make sense.

Yet most of us would think it obscene to let Susan Smith go totally unpunished for her murders. Sure, we might free Susan Smith tomorrow, on the grounds that she poses "no further threat to society." But is that the issue? Is the point of the criminal justice system simply to render Susan Smith safer to those she may encounter in the future? Or isn't the law also supposed to represent her past victims, her two dead babies? Who speaks for them? Don't they count in any system of justice worthy of the name?

Americans are a fair-minded people. They think that a criminal should be punished roughly to the extent of the harm he has caused to people—not more, and not less. This is the principle of proportionality—and most of them intuitively understand that proportionality lies at the heart of justice. That, more than anything else, is what they want, expect, and demand from the criminal justice system. But a utilitarian system, based solely on controlling future crime, invariably sacrifices justice to expediency.

Ironically, many criminal justice "hardliners," who believe in tough deterrence and incapacitation, actually share a common premise with many "bleeding hearts," who believe in rehabilitation and mercy. Hardliners typically want to impose penalties that are much more severe than the damage criminals have actually done to victims. Bleeding hearts want penalties far less severe than the damage done to victims. Both groups believe that the severity of punishments should have no necessary relationship to the seriousness of a crime. Both groups thus reject the principle of proportionality—of justice.

"The lives of predators are—by their own choice—subhuman."

Justice is a punitive response to a criminal that penalizes him in direct proportion to the harm he has done to actual individuals; to reflect back onto him the negative consequences of his criminal actions.

And this brings us back to capital punishment. The moral defense of the death penalty is the principle of justice. In the case of premeditated murder, capital punishment is the only just punishment: it is the only punishment roughly proportionate to the harm that has been done to the murder victim.

Now, anyone who respects life is understandably uneasy about taking even the lives of killers. But the principle of justice demands it, because proportionate punishment for crimes is the moral keystone of any system of justice.

If we undermine or abandon proportionality, how do we then gauge whether to punish someone for a crime, and how much? Why not a hundred lashes of the whip for stealing a loaf of bread—but a mere $5 fine for rape? We are stuck in a trap of arbitrary punishments, of different punishments for the same crime, of punishing someone either too much or too little—and of having our entire legal system lose public credibility and respect, on the grounds that it is inherently unfair and unjust. (That, in fact, is the situation our utilitarian-based legal system finds itself in today.)

To abandon proportionality in sentencing, we abandon the quest for justice itself. And to deny the death penalty for premeditated murder, is to deny the very principle of fitting punishments to offenses. If we abandon the principle of proportionality in the case of murder, the most serious of crimes, then on what grounds do we argue for proportionate punishments for any lesser crimes?

Capital Punishment Is a Moral Necessity

Capital punishment for proven premeditated murders is therefore not immoral; it is not even a "necessary evil"; *it is a moral necessity,* demanded by justice.

Critics of the death penalty—and of punishment in general—often denounce punitivity as arising from "vengeance," or some crude, vindictive notion of "an eye for an eye." But in fact, justice isn't based on revenge; it is based on retribution. The two concepts aren't the same.

The criminal (such as Pedro Medina) wants to gain something unearned and undeserved by force, at the expense of someone else (such as Dorothy James).

Retribution is the moral principle that the harm and injury imposed on the victim should be reflected proportionately back onto the criminal who caused them.

This policy is both moral and practical. Moral—because it upholds the value of innocent human life. Practical—because a policy of reflecting full harm back on the criminal frustrates his goal, which is to profit at someone else's expense. Retribution means that the criminal "won't get away with it."

The principle of proportionality also answers those critics of capital punishment who say they prefer "mercy" to "revenge." First of all, "mercy"—as these people use the term—means a negation of simple justice, by allowing the criminal to bear lower costs for his crimes than the harm he imposes on his victims. This sort of "mercy" actually encourages criminals, because they know that they can gain more from crime than any costs they will have to bear. In this respect, "mercy" (embodied in most "rehabilitation" programs) is utterly immoral.

However, one charge by death penalty opponents is true: the moral case for capital punishment does indeed rest upon making a strong distinction about the relative "worth" of human lives. The concept of justice is incompatible with the view that all human lives are "intrinsically and equally valuable," regardless of the individuals' chosen moral behavior. If that were true, then it would be wrong for an innocent victim to kill an aggressor, even in self-defense or in wartime—because the aggressor's life would be "of equal intrinsic value."

Only human predators could gain from such a policy, and only the innocent could lose. A system that would leave the morally innocent at the mercy of evil predators can be called many things, but "moral" isn't one of them.

> ***"There should be a moral statement to the guilty that there are some crimes no civilized and decent society will ever stoop to tolerate."***

On the principle of justice, only the lives of the morally innocent are truly and fully "human." The lives of predators are—by their own choice—subhuman.

A system of justice must make a clear distinction between the two—between the Pedro Medina's and the Dorothy James's of the world—and it must respond accordingly.

America was founded on the principle that each individual is an end in himself. In such a society, premeditated murder is a crime in a class by itself. Murder negates the highest moral end of civil society: the irreplaceable human life.

What possible penalty could be proportionate to such a crime, except the forfeiture of the murderer's own life?

So, in the case of premeditated murder, where there is no question of guilt and no extenuating circumstances, capital punishment should be the standard penalty—on moral grounds.

We should take no joy in the execution of predators such as Pedro Medina. The taking of a life is a symbol of the ultimate possible waste. It is a profound tragedy, which should be conducted with solemnity, dignity, and privacy. It should not become cause for public participation, celebration, or spectacle.

And it should not involve the deliberate imposition of cruelty or torture: we need not sink to the moral depths of the predators themselves. Executions should be as painless and quick as possible.

But there should be no moral apologies when capital punishment must be employed. Those occasions should be a moral affirmation to the innocent of our common commitment to justice—just as there should be a moral statement to the guilty that there are some crimes no civilized and decent society will ever stoop to tolerate.

Capital Punishment Is Reasonable

by David Gelernter

About the author: *David Gelernter is art critic at the* Weekly Standard, *Chief Scientist at Mirror Worlds Technologies Inc. (New Haven, Conn.), professor of computer science at Yale University and author of the novel* 1939 *and various other books and essays.*

No civilized nation ever takes the death penalty for granted; two recent cases force us to consider it yet again. A Texas woman, Karla Faye Tucker, murdered two people with a pickaxe, was said to have repented in prison, and was put to death. A Montana man, Theodore Kaczynski, murdered three people with mail bombs, did not repent, and struck a bargain with the Justice Department; he pleaded guilty and will not be executed. (He also attempted to murder others and succeeded in wounding some, myself included.) Why did we execute the penitent and spare the impenitent? However we answer this question, we surely have a duty to ask it.

And we ask it—I do, anyway—with a sinking feeling, because in modern America, moral upside-downness is a specialty of the house. To eliminate race prejudice we discriminate by race. We promote the cultural assimilation of immigrant children by denying them schooling in English. We throw honest citizens in jail for child abuse, relying on testimony so phony any child could see through it. Orgasm studies are okay in public high schools but the Ten Commandments are not. We make a point of admiring manly women and womanly men. None of which has anything to do with capital punishment directly, but it all obliges us to approach any question about morality in modern America in the larger context of this country's desperate confusion about elementary distinctions.

Why Execute Murderers?

Why execute murderers? To deter? To avenge? Supporters of the death penalty often give the first answer, opponents the second. But neither can be the whole truth. If our main goal were deterring crime, we would insist on public executions—which are not on the political agenda, and not an item that many Americans are interested in promoting. If our main goal were vengeance, we would allow the grieving parties to decide the murderer's fate; if the victim had no family or friends to feel vengeful on his behalf, we would call the whole thing off.

In fact, we execute murderers in order to make a communal proclamation: that murder is intolerable. A deliberate murderer embodies evil so terrible that it defiles the community. Thus the late social philosopher Robert Nisbet: "Until a catharsis has been effected through trial, through the finding of guilt and then punishment, the community is anxious, fearful, apprehensive, and above all, contaminated."

> ***"We execute murderers in order to make a communal proclamation: that murder is intolerable."***

Individual citizens have a right and sometimes a duty to speak. A community has the right, too, and sometimes the duty. The community certifies births and deaths, creates marriages, educates children, fights invaders. In laws, deeds, and ceremonies it lays down the boundary lines of civilized life, lines that are constantly getting scuffed and needing renewal.

When a murder takes place, the community is obliged, whether it feels like it or not, to clear its throat and step up to the microphone. Every murder demands a communal response. Among possible responses, the death penalty is uniquely powerful because it is permanent and can never be retracted or overturned. An execution forces the community to assume forever the burden of moral certainty; it is a form of absolute speech that allows no waffling or equivocation. Deliberate murder, the community announces, is absolutely evil and absolutely intolerable, period.

Of course, we could make the same point less emphatically if we wanted to—for example, by locking up murderers for life (as we sometimes do). The question then becomes: is the death penalty overdoing it? Should we make a less forceful proclamation instead?

The answer might be yes if we were a community in which murder was a shocking anomaly and thus in effect a solved problem. But we are not. Our big cities are full of murderers at large. "One can guesstimate," writes the criminologist and political scientist John J. DiIulio, Jr., "that we are nearing or may already have passed the day when 500,000 murderers, convicted and undetected, are living in American society."

An Old Story

DiIulio's statistics show an approach to murder so casual as to be depraved. We are reverting to a pre-civilized state of nature. Our natural bent in the face of murder is not to avenge the crime but to shrug it off, except in those rare cases when our own near and dear are involved. (And even then, it depends.)

Chapter 1

This is an old story. Cain murders Abel and is brought in for questioning: where is Abel, your brother? The suspect's response: how should I know? "What am I, my brother's keeper?" It is one of the very first statements attributed to mankind in the Bible; voiced here by an interested party, it nonetheless expresses a powerful and universal inclination. Why mess in other people's problems? And murder is always, in the most immediate sense, someone else's problem, because the injured party is dead.

Murder in primitive societies called for a private settling of scores. The community as a whole stayed out of it. For murder to count, as it does in the Bible, as a crime not merely against one man but against the whole community and against God—that was a moral triumph that is still basic to our integrity, and that is never to be taken for granted. By executing murderers, the community reaffirms this moral understanding by restating the truth that absolute evil exists and must be punished.

Granted (some people say), the death penalty is a communal proclamation; it is nevertheless an incoherent one. If our goal is to affirm that human life is more precious than anything else, how can we make such a declaration by destroying life?

But declaring that human life is more precious than anything else is not our goal in imposing the death penalty. Nor is the proposition true. The founding fathers pledged their lives (and fortunes and sacred honor) to the cause of freedom; Americans have traditionally believed that some things are more precious than life. ("Living in a sanitary age, we are getting so we place too high a value on human life—which rightfully must always come second to human ideas." Thus E.B. White in 1938, pondering the Munich pact ensuring "peace in our time" between the Western powers and Hitler.) The point of capital punishment is not to pronounce on life in general but on the crime of murder.

> ***"To believe in the sanctity of human life does not mean . . . that capital punishment is ruled out."***

Which is not to say that the sanctity of human life does not enter the picture. Taking a life, says the Talmud (in the course of discussing Cain and Abel), is equivalent to destroying a whole world. The rabbis used this statement to make a double point: to tell us why murder is the gravest of crimes, and to warn against false testimony in a murder trial. But to believe in the sanctity of human life does not mean, and the Talmud does not say it means, that capital punishment is ruled out.

Unjust Application of Capital Punishment Does Not Warrant Abolishing It

A newer objection grows out of the seemingly random way in which we apply capital punishment. The death penalty might be a reasonable communal proclamation in principle, some critics say, but it has become so garbled in practice that it has lost all significance and ought to be dropped. DiIulio writes that "the ratio of persons murdered to persons executed for murder from 1977 to 1996 was in the ballpark of 1,000 to 1"; the death penalty has become in his view "arbitrary and capricious," a "state lottery" that is "unjust both as a matter of Judeo-Christian ethics and as a matter of American citizenship."

We can grant that, on the whole, we are doing a disgracefully bad job of administering the death penalty. After all, we are divided and confused on the issue. The community at large is strongly in favor of capital punishment; the cultural elite is strongly against it. Our attempts to speak with assurance as a community come out sounding in consequence like a man who is fighting off a choke-hold as he talks. But a community as cavalier about murder as we are has no right to back down. That we are botching things does not entitle us to give up.

Opponents of capital punishment tend to describe it as a surrender to our emotions—to grief, rage, fear, blood lust. For most supporters of the death penalty, this is exactly false. Even when we resolve in principle to go ahead, we have to steel ourselves. Many of us would find it hard to kill a dog, much less a man. Endorsing capital punishment means not that we yield to our emotions but that we overcome them. (Immanuel Kant, the great advocate of the death penalty precisely on moral grounds, makes this point in his reply to the anticapital-punishment reformer Cesare Beccaria—accusing Beccaria of being "moved by sympathetic sentimentality and an affectation of humanitarianism.") If we favor executing murderers it is not because we want to but because, however much we do not want to, we consider ourselves obliged to.

Many Americans, of course, no longer feel that obligation. The death penalty is hard for us as a community above all because of our moral evasiveness. For at least a generation, we have urged one another to switch off our moral faculties. "Don't be judgmental!" We have said it so many times, we are starting to believe it.

The Refusal to Acknowledge Evil

The death penalty is a proclamation about absolute evil, but many of us are no longer sure that evil even exists. We define evil out of existence by calling it "illness"—a tendency Aldous Huxley anticipated in his novel *Brave New World* (1932) and Robert Nisbet wrote about in 1982: "America has lost the villain, the evil one, who has now become one of the sick, the disturbed. . . . America has lost the moral value of guilt, lost it to the sickroom."

Our refusal to look evil in the face is no casual notion; it is a powerful drive. Thus we have (for example) the terrorist Theodore Kaczynski, who planned and carried out a hugely complex campaign of violence with a clear goal in mind. It was the goal most terrorists have: to get famous and not die. He wanted public attention for his ideas about technology; he figured he could get it by attacking people with bombs.

He was right. His plan succeeded. It is hard to imagine a more compelling proof of mental competence than this planning and carrying out over decades of a complex, rational strategy. (Evil, yes; irrational, no; they are different things.) The man himself has said repeatedly that he is perfectly sane, knew what he was doing, and is proud of it.

To call such a man insane seems to me like deliberate perversity. But many people do. Some of them insist that his thoughts about technology constitute "delusions," though every terrorist holds strong beliefs that are wrong, and many nonterrorists do, too. Some insist that sending bombs through the mail is ipso facto proof of insanity—as if the 20th century had not taught us that there is no limit to the bestiality of which sane men are capable.

"If we favor executing murderers it is not because we want to but because, however much we do not want to, we consider ourselves obliged to."

Where does this perversity come from? I said earlier that the community at large favors the death penalty, but intellectuals and the cultural elite tend to oppose it. This is not (I think) because they abhor killing more than other people do, but because the death penalty represents absolute speech from a position of moral certainty, and doubt is the black-lung disease of the intelligentsia—an occupational hazard now inflicted on the culture as a whole.

American intellectuals have long differed from the broader community—particularly on religion, crime and punishment, education, family, the sexes, race relations, American history, taxes and public spending, the size and scope of government, art, the environment, and the military. (Otherwise, I suppose, they and the public have been in perfect accord.) But not until the late 60's and 70's were intellectuals finally in a position to act on their convictions. Whereupon they attacked the community's moral certainties with the enthusiasm of guard dogs leaping at throats. The result is an American community smitten with the disease of intellectual doubt—or, in this case, self-doubt.

The failure of our schools is a consequence of our self-doubt, of our inability to tell children that learning is not fun and they are required to master certain topics whether they want to or not. The tortured history of modern American race relations grows out of our self-doubt: we passed a civil-rights act in 1964, then lost confidence immediately in our ability to make a race-blind society work; racial preferences codify our refusal to believe in our own good faith. During the late stages of the cold war, many Americans laughed at the idea that the American way was morally superior or the Soviet Union was an "evil empire"; some are still laughing. Within their own community and the American community at large, doubting intellectuals have taken refuge (as doubters often do) in bullying, to the point where many of us are now so uncomfortable at the prospect of confronting evil that we turn away and change the subject.

Returning then to the penitent woman and the impenitent man: the Karla Faye

Tucker case is the harder of the two. We are told that she repented of the vicious murders she committed. If that is true, we would still have had no business forgiving her, or forgiving any murderer. As Dennis Prager has written apropos this case, only the victim is entitled to forgive, and the victim is silent. But showing mercy to penitents is part of our religious tradition, and I cannot imagine renouncing it categorically.

Why was Cain not put to death, but condemned instead to wander the earth forever? Among the answers given by the rabbis in the Midrash is that he repented. The moral category of repentance is so important, they said, that it was created before the world itself. I would therefore consider myself morally obligated to think long and hard before executing a penitent. But a true penitent would have to have renounced (as Karla Faye Tucker did) all legal attempts to overturn the original conviction. If every legal avenue has been tried and has failed, the penitence window is closed. Of course, this still leaves the difficult problem of telling counterfeit penitence from the real thing, but everything associated with capital punishment is difficult.

As for Kaczynski, the prosecutors who accepted the murderer's plea-bargain say they got the best outcome they could, under the circumstances, and I believe them. But I also regard this failure to execute a cold-blooded impenitent terrorist murderer as a tragic abdication of moral responsibility. The tragedy lies in what, under our confused system, the prosecutors felt compelled to do. The community was called on to speak unambiguously. It flubbed its lines, shrugged its shoulders, and walked away.

Which brings me back to our moral condition as a community. I can describe our plight better in artistic than in philosophical terms. The most vivid illustrations I know of self-doubt and its consequences are the paintings and sculptures of Alberto Giacometti (who died in 1966). Giacometti was an artist of great integrity; he was consumed by intellectual and moral self-doubt, which he set down faithfully. His sculpted figures show elongated, shriveled human beings who seem corroded by acid, eaten-up to the bone, hurt and weakened past fragility nearly to death. They are painful to look at. And they are natural emblems of modern America. We ought to stick one on top of the Capitol and think it over.

"Communities may exist in which capital punishment is no longer the necessary response to deliberate murder. America today is not one of them."

In executing murderers, we declare that deliberate murder is absolutely evil and absolutely intolerable. This is a painfully difficult proclamation for a self-doubting community to make. But we dare not stop trying. Communities may exist in which capital punishment is no longer the necessary response to deliberate murder. America today is not one of them.

Capital Punishment Is Not Barbaric

by Don Feder

About the author: *Don Feder is a nationally syndicated columnist.*

Opponents of the death penalty have made an astonishing discovery—execution hurts. Armed with this vital information, they hope to win over the 75 to 80 percent of us who support capital punishment.

They are convinced that recent executions in Utah and Delaware—one by firing squad, the other by hanging—will strengthen their case. Lethal injection is said to be antiseptic. It doesn't fully convey the horror of the state taking a human life.

But the brutality of these archaic forms of execution cannot fail to change the public's mind, bleeding hearts bleated.

"The first reaction is disbelief," says Bill Breedlove of the National Coalition to Abolish the Death Penalty. "People are disgusted by it."

The media help the cause. Stories focused on how many minutes had passed before Billy Bailey (hanged in Delaware for the shotgun slaying of an elderly couple) was pronounced dead. We were treated to graphic accounts of bullets ripping into the body of John Albert Taylor, convicted of the murder-rape of an 11-year-old girl.

Michael Rushford, president of the Criminal Justice Legal Foundation (a counter-ACLU) was not moved. "Most of us, who will eventually die a lingering death in a nursing home, won't go as easily as these killers," he observed.

"People really don't care if a murderer is hanged or shot," Rushford added. Some were doubtless overjoyed that Taylor faced a firing squad and probably wouldn't have minded if he'd got it one shot at a time, starting with the knees—particularly if they were familiar with his crime.

Consider the Suffering of Victims and Survivors

Whatever Taylor experienced in his final moments, it was nothing next to the anguish of his victim. Described as a "remorseless pedophile," Taylor stalked 11-year-old Charla Nicole King. When he found her alone in her mother's

Reprinted from "Pity the Poor Killers, Execution Hurts," by Don Feder, *Conservative Chronicle*, February 14, 1996, by permission of Don Feder and Creators Syndicate.

home, he tore off the child's clothes, stuffed her underpants in her mouth, raped her and strangled her with a telephone cord.

"We will never know the agony, the fear and the suffering that Charla King endured," prosecutor Reed Richards told the court in his closing argument. Richards believes the child's ordeal may have lasted an hour and a half. She died one day before her 12th birthday.

After robbing a liquor store and getting wired on booze and pills, Bailey murdered Gilbert Lambertson, 80, and his wife, Clara, age 73. The man's face was blown off. His wife saw him die before Bailey turned the shotgun on her.

The suffering of their victims was only the beginning of the misery Taylor and Bailey inflicted. For the survivors, the anguish never ends.

"Whatever [rapist and murderer John] Taylor experienced in his final moments, it was nothing next to the anguish of his victim."

Charla's family raised her for 12 years—loved her, cared for her, watched her take her first baby steps, heard her laughter, saw the pictures she painted in school, dreamed of her future as she trembled on the brink of adolescence. All of this ended in 90 minutes of misery at the hands of a creature whose continued existence was an affront to humanity.

"They say executing him is so barbaric," shrugged Sherron King, mother of the murdered child. "Tell me what's barbaric. My daughter was alive (while being raped and choked). He won't even hear the sound of the bullets."

"This should have been done 15 years ago (at the time of the murders)," said Mark Moore, grandson of the Lambertsons. "There were too many appeals. My grandparents had no appeals."

In February 1996, the families of those who died in the 1995 Oklahoma City bombing lobbied Congress to expedite the execution of convicted killers.

"This bill has got to be passed," pleaded Alice Maroney, whose father, a Secret Service agent, died in the explosion. "It's not whether you are a Republican or a Democrat, it's whether you have a heart." Her appeal is the proper application of compassion to the capital punishment debate.

"Why do we kill people who kill people to teach people that killing people is wrong?" muses the American Civil Liberty Union's Nadine Strossen.

Most of us don't need to be taught that murder is wrong. We kill those who rape and murder little girls so they will rape and murder little girls no more. (Life in prison without the possibility of parole is an illusion.) And because it's the only fitting punishment for so horrendous an act.

My friend Tom Landess, who used to teach English at the University of Dallas, swears that when various forms of execution were being debated before the Texas legislature, an old Democrat stood up and harrumphed: "Lethal injection? Why that's no more than a slap on the wrist!" As the Aussies say, good on you, mate.

The State Has a Right to Execute Violent Criminals

by Deal Hudson

About the author: *Deal Hudson is the editor and publisher of* Crisis, *a monthly Roman Catholic periodical.*

The popular film *Dead Man Walking* sent more than a few ripples through the country on the topic of the death penalty. Despite the film's well-taken point about God's mercy, its sentimental appeal only convinced me that most arguments against the death penalty are ill-founded.

Not the overt emotional plea, the gruesomeness of the execution itself, or the film's attempt—through the eyes of Sr. Helen Prejean—to humanize the killer shook my confidence in the state's right to execute its most flagrant criminals.

The pope's 1999 plea to "have mercy on [death-row criminal] Mr. Mease," whispered in the ear of Missouri's governor, unexpectedly shook me. The differences between the film and the pope's witness are many, some obvious, but the one that struck me was its cool, moral logic.

Capital Punishment Is Not an Intrinsic Evil

Bear in mind what the pope *did not say:* He did not question the state's right to impose the death penalty, as clearly stated in the *Catechism of the Catholic Church.* He did not say the death penalty was an intrinsic evil, on a moral par with abortion and euthanasia.

The pope's argument, in short, is not against the death penalty but against the use of the death penalty. This distinction has been obscured, and will continue to be, in the media discussions of the pope's 1999 visit to the U.S.

Our Holy Father is leaving untouched the Catholic teaching on the death penalty. However, he is asking the state to refrain from exercising its right because he believes the state can guarantee the safety of its citizens by keeping dangerous criminals locked up.

Five arguments can be employed in defense of the pope's position:

Reprinted, with permission, from "Mercy for Mr. Mease," by Deal Hudson, Sed Contra column, *Crisis*, March 1999.

- A murderer should be given as much time as possible to undergo *spiritual* reform.
- The death penalty is a punishment that cannot be retracted if new evidence proves innocence.
- The death penalty is a punishment, not an act of revenge, and should be viewed without that motive.
- The modern state has tragically abused its power over life and death making it preferable that the state exercise that power as little as possible.
- In a culture of death, the option for the death penalty, although morally licit, should be rejected by Catholics as a witness to their belief in the sacredness of all human life.

The pope's practical advice suggests that the death penalty should not be used to patch up a criminal justice system that leaks murderers back into society. Systemic problems, like over-crowding or expense, should not prevent a life sentence from being carried to full term. The courts, sentences, and jails must be fixed so that those who have intentionally taken a human life can live out their days apart from civilized society.

For myself, I have made a promise to reconsider my support for using the death penalty, but to do so, I need to know the answers to these questions:

- Is the life sentence for first degree murder genuine in the 50 states, or are these sentences cut short by parole?
- Assuming there is additional expense for these life sentences, can that expense be offset in any way?
- Are life sentences adequately punitive?

The power of the pope's plea for mercy ultimately goes back to the force behind the basic question: Can we protect ourselves from these criminals without putting them to death? . . .

There are some who will be concerned that the pope's logic will ultimately lead to pacifism. Some mistakenly point to pacifism as being at the root of the pope's and the bishop's opposition to the bombing of Iraq, but neither their stand against the death penalty nor their position on the bombing affects Catholic just-war theory at all. You don't need pacifist instincts to see the political subtext in President Bill Clinton's decision to bomb.

Neither does a reconsideration of the death penalty lead to the faulty reasoning of the "seamless garment." [The "seamless garment" refers to a 1983 proposal by Cardinal Joseph Bernardin for the Catholic Church to promote a consistent, life-defending philosophy in its approach to abortion, euthanasia, capital punishment, and similar issues.] The American bishops recently threw out those tattered rags and replaced them with the image of a "house of life." This house contains many rooms: All of them are devoted to issues of life and death; none of them are tied together by the false logic of moral equivalency. Catholics can safely revisit the room of the death penalty without feeling they are aiding and abetting those in the Church who see no difference between killing an innocent life and executing those who kill in cold blood.

Capital Punishment Is Not Morally Justified

by Mark Costanzo

About the author: *Mark Costanzo is the author of* Just Revenge, *from which this viewpoint is excerpted.*

When faced with compelling evidence that the death penalty is costly, arbitrary, discriminatory, prone to error, and without deterrent value, retentionists often retreat into the murky waters of moral philosophy. They argue that capital punishment is not only morally legitimate, but also morally necessary. Although we can decide questions of fact—questions about cost, deterrence, fairness, and public opinion—by analyzing the relevant data, the question of whether the death penalty is ethically justified cannot be answered by any amount of data. It is a matter of faith and argument. And that is precisely why many supporters of the death penalty would prefer to debate philosophy instead of effectiveness. If we are morally compelled to kill those who kill, further discussion of troublesome facts is irrelevant and unnecessary. Questions about how the death penalty is administered, about the cost or the consequences of the penalty may be interesting, but they do not have the power to refute a moral imperative.

The philosophical arguments surrounding capital punishment are based on religious authority, moral philosophy, criminal responsibility, and concern for victims.

The Bible Tells Me So

In their final appeals to jurors, prosecutors in capital murder trials are fond of quoting Scripture to lend authority to their arguments. And there are many verses to choose from. In particular, the Old Testament seems to suggest killing as a response to a variety of crimes. The most popular quotation is from Deuteronomy (19:21): "Life for life, eye for eye, tooth for tooth, hand for hand, foot for foot." Moreover, the Old Testament recommends death for an assortment of crimes, including murder, contempt for parental authority, defiling sacred places or objects, kidnapping for ransom, sorcery, bestiality, worshiping

Excerpted from *Just Revenge: Costs and Consequences of the Death Penalty*, by Mark Costanzo.

false gods, profaning the Sabbath, adultery, incest, homosexuality, blasphemy, bearing false witness in court, harlotry, negligence that results in a death, and false prophesy.

Yet, despite the apparent biblical endorsement of executions, there is much even in the Old Testament to suggest that killing may not be the appropriate penalty for murder. God did not kill Cain for the murder of Abel, and several cities of refuge were established so that wrongdoers could escape vengeance at the hands of the victims' families. The idea that "vengeance belongs to the Lord" and that we should "love our neighbor as ourselves" are major themes of the Old Testament. Even the often misinterpreted "eye for an eye" passage was meant to *restrain* rather than to *require* vengeance. Religious scholars point out that, taken in context, the passage does not tell us that we must exact proportional revenge, but that we may not take from others more than has been taken from us, that we must resist the urge to retaliate with ever greater violence. *Lex talionis*, the doctrine of legal retaliation, represented an advance, a movement away from unrestrained retaliation.

"There is much even in the Old Testament to suggest that killing may not be the appropriate penalty for murder."

Though the Old Testament authorizes executions in principle, in practice, according to legal scholars R.J. Tabak and M. Lane, "there were such extensive procedural requirements for the imposition of the death penalty that, by design, it was nearly impossible to secure a death verdict." Mosaic law and, later, the Rabbinic tradition established a nearly unreachable standard of proof. In the Talmudic courts (called Sanhedrins) two witnesses judged to be competent had to testify that they saw the accused commit the crime after being forewarned that the act was illegal and punishable by death. Confessions were inadmissible. So was testimony against the defendant by family members of the victim or persons with a preexisting grievance against the defendant. If any aspect of the evidence or testimony was found to be unreliable, the defendant could not be killed. Such restrictions served to make capital punishment extremely rare under Talmudic law.

For Christians, the Old Testament must be interpreted in light of the New Testament, which goes much farther in repudiating revenge: "You have heard that it was said, 'An eye for an eye and a tooth for a tooth.' But I say to you, do not resist one who is evil. But if any one strikes you on the right cheek, turn to him the other also" (Matthew 5:38–41). The New Testament emphasizes love, compassion, mercy, charity, forgiveness. And, if we are to follow the example of Christ, forgiveness and compassion are especially important when dealing with criminals and outcasts. When Christ was confronted with a woman convicted of adultery (a capital crime at the time), the crowd who had assembled to stone her asked, "Teacher, this woman hath been taken in adultery, in the very act. Now the law of Moses commanded us to stone such: What then sayest thou of her?" In response, Jesus "lifted up himself and said unto them, 'He that is without sin among you, let him cast the first stone'" (John 8:3–11). The same message can be found in Luke: "Judge not and you will not be judged; condemn not, and you will not be condemned; forgive, and you will be forgiven" (6:37). The entire life and teachings of Jesus argue against killing as a form of punishment. Though not a theologian, Charles Dickens made the point well:

> Though every other man who wields a pen should turn himself into a commentator on the scriptures—not all their united efforts could persuade me that executions are a Christian law. . . . If any text appeared to justify the claim, I would reject that limited appeal, and rest upon the character of the Redeemer and the great scheme of His religion.

Although the Bible can be read to support the death penalty, this support is subject to severe restrictions. Specifically, guilt must be certain and execution must be necessary to serve the interests of justice (e.g., to protect others or to instill respect for moral authority). Indeed, no less an authority than Pope John Paul II has observed that the necessary requirements for the death penalty are seldom, if ever, met. In "Evangelium Vitae" (The Gospel of Life) the pope argues that "as explicitly formulated, the precept 'You shall not kill' is strongly negative: it indicates the extreme limit which can never be exceeded." John Paul II goes on to note that punishment

"Religious organizations are nearly unanimous in their condemnation of capital punishment."

> ought not go to the extreme of executing the offender except in cases of absolute necessity: in other words, when it would not be possible otherwise to defend society. Today, however, as a result of steady improvements in the organization of the penal system, such cases are very rare, if not practically nonexistent. . . . If bloodless means are sufficient to defend human lives against an aggressor and to protect public order and the safety of persons, public authority must limit itself to such means.

The pope is not a lone voice among religious leaders. Religious organizations are nearly unanimous in their condemnation of capital punishment. More than forty such organizations (including American Baptists, Catholics, Episcopalians, Jews, Lutherans, Mennonites, Methodists, Presbyterians, Quakers, and Unitarians) have issued statements calling for the abolition of capital punishment.

Moral Philosophy and the Functions of Punishment

When measured against the usual standards for evaluating punishment, the death penalty doesn't make much sense. Obviously, killing a prisoner eliminates the possibility of rehabilitation; a corpse cannot go on to lead a more virtuous life. The goal of incapacitation is not advanced: the condemned man is already safely behind prison walls, unable to commit further crimes in free society. The supposed deterrent effect is illusory: executions appear actually to *increase* the level of violence in society. And since incapacitation and protection of society are just as effectively—and more cheaply—achieved through life imprisonment, killing the prisoner is simply unnecessary.

Moreover, how does the notion of killing murderers square with the cherished principle of "the sanctity of human life"? This idea is central to the world's great religions as well as the ancient Greek, Egyptian, Persian, and Babylonian moral philosophers. If life is sacred, it means that every person has the right to live simply by virtue of the fact that he or she is a living, breathing human being. This right is unearned and inalienable, in part because we are created "in the image of God." This basic principle certainly implies that the death penalty is morally wrong. However, three centuries ago, John Locke offered a classic defense of the death penalty on moral grounds. He argued that although the right to life is inherent and absolute, it is possible to "forfeit" one's right to life by committing a crime that "deserves death." His arguments have provided ammunition for supporters of capital punishment ever since. Locke also argued for severe punishment on the grounds of deterrence. He believed that we should punish "to the degree and with as much severity, as will suffice to make it an ill bargain to the offender, give him cause to repent, and terrify others from doing the like.

Another influential moral argument is usually traced to Immanuel Kant. He believed that murderers must be killed based on the principle of "equal" or "just" retribution:

> What kind and what degree of punishment does public legal justice adopt as its principle and standard? None other than the principle of equality . . . any undeserved evil that you inflict on someone else among the people is one that you do to yourself. . . . Only the law of retribution can determine exactly the kind and degree of punishment.

This idea has an elegant and appealing simplicity. It is an elaboration of the idea of *lex talionis* and is similar to the argument that murderers must be "paid back" in kind for their crimes. The principle of equality introduced by Kant seems to provide a standard that is independent of religious or political authority. And whereas Locke linked his notion of retribution to deterrence, Kant apparently felt that such practical considerations were not important enough to discuss.

> ***"If killing is morally wrong, it is wrong for both the individual and the state."***

Another argument offered in defense of the idea that justice requires the killing of murderers might be called the "moral solidarity" argument. If societies are held together, in part, by a shared consensus of what constitutes immoral behavior, then those who violate the moral order must be punished to restore moral balance in society. Further, for murderers, any punishment less than death is too weak to convey the strong sense of outrage and condemnation felt by the community. Only by killing the murderer can we repair the moral integrity of the larger community. In his book *For Capital Punishment,* Walter Berns puts it like this:

> [The death penalty] serves to remind us of the majesty of the moral order that is embodied in our law and of the terrible consequences of breach. . . . The criminal law must be made awful, by which I mean awe-inspiring, or commanding "profound respect or reverential fear." It must remind us of the moral order by which alone we can live as human beings.

These arguments raise several questions. If by killing, murderers forfeit their right to live, does that mean that we are, in turn, *obliged* to kill them? Or will other forms of severe punishment suffice? If someone *deserves* to die, does it mean that we have the right to kill him? Should we try to induce in prisoners the equivalent amount of suffering they induced in their victims? Do executions really strengthen the moral solidarity of the community, or do they demean and corrupt the collective morality? Should executions be bloody, excruciating, and public to fully inspire awe and "reverential fear"? Is it necessary to kill in order to show that killing is wrong? And given the varied backgrounds and capacities of defendants, the diverse types of murder, and the limits of human understanding, is it even possible to decide fairly which murderers deserve to die?

Unnecessary Killing Is Always Wrong

The simplest counterargument is that, if killing is morally wrong, it is wrong for both the individual and the state. To be sure, there are circumstances where killing may be necessary, for example, when a police officer shoots a robber who is about to kill a clerk, when a soldier kills an enemy soldier during a time of war, when a woman shoots a violently abusive husband who is coming toward her brandishing a knife. These situations involve imminent danger, split-second decisions, and self-defense or defense of innocent others. Unlike police officers, who occasionally kill to protect their own lives or the lives of innocent people, the executioner performs an unnecessary killing, a killing that has nothing to do with self-defense, imminent danger, or the protection of society. The murderer has already been captured and waits in a prison cell safely isolated from the community.

The law of equal retribution proposed by Kant and others cannot be a literal prescription for how to punish violent criminals. We would find it morally repugnant to torture torturers, rape rapists, or terrorize terrorists. We do not try to kill murderers using the same method they used to kill their victims. Instead, we imprison them. Our efforts to mitigate punishments arise out of the recognition that we must not sink to the level of the criminal; raping a rapist would debase us, weaken our moral solidarity, and undermine the moral authority of the state. We cannot simply respond to cruelty with our own acts of cruelty. Acts of brutality committed by the state in the name of justice never ennoble us. There must be severe punishment for horrible crimes, but that does not oblige us to kill those who have killed.

Try as we might, we can never sever the ties between moral concerns and practical realities. *Morality can only be assessed in practice.* Even if we accept the morality of the death penalty in the abstract, we must always look at how it is administered in the real world. Is the death penalty still moral if innocent people are sometimes convicted or executed? Is it still moral if the race of the murderer or the victim plays a substantial role in determining which defendants will be sentenced to die? Is it still moral if the ultimate penalty squanders money that could be more productively spent on preventing crime? Is it still moral if executions provoke, rather than deter, violent criminals? These questions must be answered before any final judgment can be made about the morality of the death penalty. Moral theory must give way to moral practice, and abstract benefits must be balanced against tangible costs. Defenders of capital punishment must defend this punishment *as it exists* in the real world. . . .

"There must be severe punishment for horrible crimes, but that does not oblige us to kill those who have killed."

Just Revenge

Beneath the usual justifications for punishing criminals lurks a more visceral and potent motive for the death penalty: revenge. The desire to lash back at those who have harmed us has deep roots in our evolutionary past. It is a powerful human motive that must be taken seriously, but it is not a sufficient justification for killing. Although individually we all feel the primitive urge to exact revenge against those who harm us, collectively we must strive to be more rational, fair, moral, and humane than the criminals who commit the acts of violence or cruelty that we condemn. We all sympathize with a bereaved father who attempts to kill the man who murdered his child. But a group's craving for revenge is far less innocent and immediate, and far less justifiable. A victim's relative who attempts to kill a murderer commits a crime of passion motivated by rage and grief. In contrast, the process leading up to a state-sponsored killing is slow, deliberate, methodical, and largely stripped of human emotion. The anger of families of victims is understandable, but anger should not be the basis of social policy. A community's angry cry for killing a murderer is far uglier than the anger felt by an individual who has been wronged by another.

We have all felt wronged and we have all experienced the powerful emotions that drive the hunger for revenge. The urge to see a murderer killed is rooted in the rage and revulsion that most Americans feel when they hear about a horrible, inexplicable murder. We empathize with the victim and the family of the victim, and we want to see the murderer pay dearly for his or her crime. In movies, operas, plays, and novels, exacting revenge on those who offend us is often portrayed as emotionally satisfying. But just because the appetite for revenge is real and powerful, that does not mean we should indulge our appetite or build it into our legal system. Justice must take precedence over revenge. Arthur Koestler made this point vividly: "Deep inside every civilized being there lurks a tiny Stone Age man, dangling a club to rob and rape, and screaming 'an eye for an eye.' But we would rather not have that little fur-clad figure dictate the law of the land." Feelings of anger and revulsion at a horrible crime are understandably human and maybe even a healthy indication of concern for the welfare of others. However, even if we accept the legitimacy of anger, anger does not outweigh all other considerations. Feelings of outrage and the quest for revenge do not guarantee that punishments will be fairly or rationally imposed. Anger does not ensure justice; it is an obstacle to justice.

It would be immoral to execute everyone who kills another human being. Every legal system on earth recognizes this. Consequently, every nation with capital punishment must create some method of selecting out those killers who truly "deserve" to die. Because no selection process is perfect, bias, prejudice, and error creep into every system of capital punishment. If the morality of revenge and the morality of the death penalty are to be defended, the defense must be of the death penalty as it is administered in the real world. Too often, defenders of the death penalty argue for its morality in a theoretical, idealized world. The claim that killing is morally justified must be reconciled with disquieting facts: the inevitability of wrongful convictions, the reality of discrimination on the basis of wealth and race, the likelihood that executions increase the murder rate, the reality that millions of dollars must be squandered to bring about a single execution.

"Is the death penalty still moral if innocent people are sometimes convicted or executed?"

Killing is a morally acceptable penalty only if it is essential, and only if it provides substantial benefits that cannot be gained by any other means. Capital punishment is not just a moral abstraction. It is a reality that must be evaluated on the basis of benefits and costs.

Execution Is Inhumane

by Robert Johnson

About the author: *Robert Johnson is Professor of Justice, Law, and Society in the School of Public Affairs at American University in Washington, D.C. He is also the author of several books, including* Condemned to Die: Life under Sentence of Death, *and* Death Work: A Study of the Modern Execution Process.

America, perhaps more than any other country, has tinkered with the mechanics of legal executions in a search for the "perfect" method. In operational terms, perfect means the most tame and reliable method of killing made possible by existing technology. Our preferred methods have evolved over the centuries. Beginning with the rather simple and unambiguous violence of hangings and shootings (by firing squads)—which involved direct and unembellished applications of techniques used elsewhere in the world and, in the case of hangings, in practice for centuries—we moved on to the relatively complicated but more tame killings made possible by twentieth-century technology: the gas chamber, the electric chair, and most recently, lethal injection. In a sense, our history lives on in today's execution methods, since each is still in use since the advent of the contemporary death penalty in 1976. In descending order of frequency, at year's end 1996, there have been a total of 223 executions by lethal injection, 128 by electrocution, 10 by gas, 4 by hanging, and 2 by firing squad. If we look back over the twentieth century as a whole, the predominant method has been the electric chair, which has taken well over four thousand lives. The method of the future would appear to be lethal injection. Presently authorized in thirty-two states—in contrast to electrocution, authorized today in only eleven—lethal injection is far and away the most frequently used method these days and for the foreseeable future. Executions by either of the two most common methods today, lethal injection or electrocution, share an important feature: each lends itself to impersonal bureaucratic procedures and the appearance of quick, bloodless, and even painless deaths.

Is Execution Painless?

Today we have an elaborate and largely clandestine bureaucracy to carry out death sentences, and we use technologically sophisticated modes of execution.

The changes are telling. Slowly but inexorably we have distanced ourselves from the reality of the death penalty. We now kill efficiently and, above all, impersonally—"without anger or passion," to use Max Weber's fine phrase—like so many functionaries in the business of justice. The contemporary execution procedure is unlike any of the premodern procedures—even those followed in executions at the turn of the twentieth century. Though modern executions are obviously violent in that they entail the forcible taking of life, the technical process is typically quick, clean, and precise, and ostensibly free of physical pain. Such, then, is the nature of progress. We have come a long way from the public slaughters of the past.

> ***"Lethal injection [and] electrocution share an important feature: each lends itself to impersonal bureaucratic procedures and the appearance of quick, bloodless, and even painless deaths."***

Or have we? We normally think of modern execution methods as humane because they are physically painless. Certainly these methods appear painless, but appearances can be misleading. H.E. Barnes, for example, has cited anecdotal evidence from earlier in this century that casts doubt on the presumed painlessness of electrocution, which has been the most common method of execution in use in America in the twentieth century." More recently, R.W. Denno has marshalled an impressive array of scientific evidence on this subject that, once again, raises the unsettling prospect that, despite disclaimers by some experts and executioners, and despite the comparatively tame execution scene associated with the electric chair, "death by electrocution may inflict 'unnecessary pain,' physical violence, and 'mutilation'" in violation of the Eighth Amendment.

Electrocutions are probably painful, and may be excruciatingly so. We now know that the considerable electricity generated by the chair largely circumvents the brain, which is insulated by the skull, and instead passes through the body and out the leg. Thus, while massive surges of electricity are coursing through his body, the prisoner is almost certainly conscious; nerve activity—which carries the sensation of pain—remains intact. We have convinced ourselves that prisoners don't experience pain in large part because they do not move or speak, which of course would be natural reactions to pain. But prisoners in the throes of electrocution do not move or speak because they are physically paralyzed; they can only sit, frozen and mute, in an enduring painful spasm. In the words of Harold Hillman, a neurobiologist,

> It is usually thought that the failure of the convict to move is a sign that he cannot feel pain. He cannot move because all of his muscles are contracted maximally. A physiological effect that in itself is enormously painful and further prevents the prisoner from crying out or providing other outward signs of other massively painful effects of electrocution such as third degree burns and an enormous heating up of the bodily fluids throughout the body. . . . While

> the subject remains conscious, strapped into the chair, paralyzed yet aware of the gruesome burning of his body, it is scientifically and medically certain that death is not instantaneous.

Things are almost certainly worse when electrocutions are botched. Then, electricity must be applied more frequently; sometimes electrocutions take up to fifteen minutes to finally kill the prisoner. Over the twentieth century, about one out of every nine or ten electrocutions has been botched. (Public executions were probably botched at a much higher rate, at least judging by anecdotal accounts.) We may expect more botchings in the coming years. Most electric chairs are old. Poor electrode connections, the most common cause of botched electrocutions, will if anything grow more common as electric chairs deteriorate.

Modern Hangings and the Gas Chamber

It is chilling to think that the very measures we have used to assure ourselves that modern executions are tame and hence painless may in fact be profoundly misleading. As it happens, even modern, proficient hangings—the kind seemingly over in seconds, producing a hangman's fracture and a quietly dangling body—are likely to be painful. We tend to think otherwise, once again, because most of these hanging victims are paralyzed, not unconscious, and strangle to death unable to move or otherwise express pain. Earlier hangings, for example in the Middle Ages or in the American South, produced visibly painful strangulations replete with people struggling for life. In such instances, the pain and indignity were seen as proper features of an execution. A modern hanging, in contrast, *looks* like a good, clean kill by a master craftsman. Syd Dernley, the modern English hangman, maintained that not only were his hangings quick—over in seconds—but painless. "Certainly he suffered no pain," contended Dernley, referring to the typical prisoner hanged in a twentieth-century English prison. Dernley may have been wrong on both counts. The hanged man may have lingered for minutes, not seconds, and suffered considerable pain. Prisoners are not cut down, in the case of hanging, or otherwise removed from the execution apparatus until a "decent interval" has passed. Whatever may be the motivation for this decorous pause in an otherwise brutal execution ritual, one effect is to maintain the appearance that death is quick and painless. By the time we remove the body of the condemned from the execution apparatus, any evidence of life or pain in death has passed from the scene.

"Death by electrocution may inflict 'unnecessary pain,' physical violence, and 'mutilation' in violation of the Eighth Amendment."

Former Supreme Court Justice Brennan, in his eloquent dissent from denial of certiorari in *Glass v. Louisiana*, made a compelling case for the violence of electrocution, which he maintained was a clear violation of the Eighth Amendment. In that same dissent, Brennan cited evidence that criminals executed in the gas chamber—by asphyxiation—suffered great pain over a number of minutes; that method, too, Brennan concluded, was a violation of the Eighth Amendment. The gas chamber was meant to be a successor to the electric chair. There was no mutilation of the body; no powerful surge of raw electrical power. Gas was thought to kill quickly and quietly. Few states adopted this method, however. It was expensive—a gas chamber is a fairly elaborate technical undertaking, requiring considerable upkeep. The mechanics of execution by lethal gas are comparatively complex. There is also an element of danger; lethal gas can leak from the chamber, endangering witnesses, or can kill anyone who enters the chamber before it has been properly cleared. The gas chamber may have fallen into disfavor because of the association of lethal gas with the genocidal campaigns of the Nazis in World War II, which occurred shortly after the first American gas chambers were put in place. Perhaps most important, prisoners in the gas chamber appeared to suffocate in a slow and painful way, though again, some experts wrote off these reactions—including head-banging, drooling, gasping for air, and even moaning—as postmortem responses rather than death agonies. In a 1994 case, *Fierro v. Gomez*, the United States District Court for the Northern District of California reviewed evidence on the effects of the gas chamber and supported Justice Brennan's Eighth Amendment claim. The court "concluded that the time it takes for the lethal gas to kill an inmate combined with the degree of pain inflicted on the inmate warrants the use of another method of execution."

Lethal Injection

Most executions today are carried out by lethal injection, clearly the tamest and most apparently painless method of execution yet devised. Here, too, however, controversy reigns. Some anesthesiologists question whether lethal injection is as painless as it appears, contending that it may, like hangings, produce a paralysis that masks a slow and painful death by suffocation. In *Chaney v. Heckler,* the court referred to "known evidence concerning lethal injection which strongly indicates that such drugs pose a substantial threat of torturous pain to persons being executed." The court noted that, when using the mixture of barbiturates and paralytics required by law, "even a small error in dosage or administration can leave a prisoner conscious but paralyzed while dying, a sentient witness of his or her own slow, lingering asphyxiation." Such dosage errors would, therefore, produce botched executions. Other problems emerge as well, falling under the heading of botches or glitches. For example, it is often hard to locate veins in which to insert the needle on offenders with long histories of drug use, a category that includes many, if not most, condemned prisoners today. At other times, there have been malfunctions of medical equipment. Even in a properly administered execution by lethal injection, the prisoner has a long and emotionally painful wait while strapped to the gurney—sometimes upwards of an hour.

Lethal injection, then, offers a paradoxical execution scene. A supine inmate, seemingly at rest, appears to drift off into a sleep that merges imperceptibly with death. This is, in its essentials, the ideal modern death—a death that occurs in one's sleep, painlessly. The reality may well be completely different. The interval on the gurney, reminiscent of rest but actually a case of forced restraint, can certainly be considered a kind of torture of its own; and once the drugs are introduced, what follows may well be a death by slow suffocation—likewise, a kind of torture. All of this unfolds before us as we congratulate ourselves on our humaneness and, more macabre still, as the immobilized offender comes to realize the deception of execution by lethal injection and, unable to struggle, recognizes his inability to communicate his distress to the world. He may endure a final insult to his dignity in the form of an experience of complete and utter helplessness while others smile benignly, as if all is well with a world that kills heinous murderers with such kindness.

Pain is subjective, and it is impossible to know with certainty the experience—or range of experiences—of those who undergo execution. No one can come back from the dead to tell us about executions. Botched executions, where the offender lingers on before death, do not offer opportunities for us to assess the experience. The Francis case, where the chair failed and he lived to be executed another day, is of no help because the chair did not administer electricity of any magnitude, and hence his experience sheds no light on actual executions. Since we cannot know for sure, we must acknowledge that it is *possible* that modern executions are painless or at least comparatively pain-free, as maintained by many advocates of modern execution methods from the electric chair to lethal injection. Certainly, one can envision a lethal injection process in which the anesthetic used, in nature and amount, is such that no consciousness of physical pain is possible—much like an overdose of an anesthetic. This still leaves unexamined the *psychology* of modern executions. Here the crucial point is that, though restrained by historical standards, today's executions, even if largely or even entirely free of physical pain, are *purely destructive* undertakings that can and should be rejected on that ground alone. . . .

A Dehumanizing Process

The impersonality of the modern death penalty makes it distinctively brutal. Admittedly, this is a curious proposition. We explicitly seek humane executions. Whereas in times past we physically assaulted the condemned as a community or selected executioners brutal enough to kill them before our eyes, today we select personnel for execution teams who are, among other things, civil and accommodating to the needs of the prisoners during their last hours. To be sure, we do not pick such men, nowadays referred to as deathwatch or execution team officers, entirely out of the goodness of our hearts. Their interpersonal skills promote a decent sort of social control and facilitate the smooth execution drill that is the hallmark of the modern death penalty. Perhaps the prisoners sense that there is an element of duplicity in this, however well-meaning it may be. Though most of the condemned appreciate the attention of the deathwatch officers, both they and the officers remain emotionally aloof from one another. The result is a civil but impersonal proceeding that gives company but not comfort to the condemned.

"Even a small error in dosage [during lethal injection] . . . can leave a prisoner conscious but paralyzed while dying, a sentient witness of his or her own slow, lingering asphyxiation."

Executions today are disturbingly, even chillingly, dispassionate. If you doubt this, listen to Caryl Chessman's fictional rendering of a modern execution. Himself a death row inmate, Chessman vividly depicted the pain of a lonely, anonymous death, a death predicated on one's personal insignificance. Though fictional, even melodramatic, his account is authentic. Chessman knew, as we all know, that death is a profoundly personal experience. He knew as well that today's condemned prisoner suffers the ignominy of an impersonal death inflicted by faceless bureaucrats. This prisoner is reduced to the status of an object and disposed of according to a schedule.

> Your waiting is over.
>
> Three of the executioner's assistants come for you. The cell door is unlocked, opened. You're told quietly, impersonally, "It's time."
>
> It's time to die, to be executed.
>
> You stand there for an instant, unmoving. Perhaps you take a last drag on your cigarette, drop the butt, step on it. Three pairs of eyes watch you.
>
> "Go to hell!" you scream defiantly. "I'm not going! Do you bastards hear me? I'm not going!"
>
> They hear you. But you're going nevertheless. They'll take you by force if necessary. They have a job to do.
>
> You can whimper. You can cry out to God to help you, to save your life. But don't expect a miracle. He won't intervene. So ask only for the strength to die like a man.
>
> You can shrug. You didn't think it would come to this, but it did. And here you are, at the end of life's road, about to take that last short walk.
>
> Automatically your legs move. You're walking, mechanically—out through the death watch cell entrance, around the bend in the short hallway, through a doorway. And there it is. The gas chamber. No stopping now. No turning back. You're hustled into this squat, octagonal, glass and metal-sided cell within a room. Its elaborate gadgets don't interest you. Quickly you find yourself seated in the chair. The guards strip you down. Their movements are swift and sure, smoothly rehearsed. The stethoscope is connected.

Capital Punishment

There! The job is done.

"Good luck," says the guard captain in charge.

Then you're alone. The guards have left. The metal door has closed. The spoked wheel on the outside of that door is being given a final turn.

Everything is in readiness! This is the dreadful, final moment. While the physical preparations were underway, while you moved, it wasn't so real. Activity blocked full realization. It was like watching a gripping scene in a movie, where the camera had been speeded up and the action had carried you along with it, irresistibly. You had only a blurred awareness that it was leading to this. But now that you're physically immobilized, there's a jarring change. The camera slows. You see; you absorb; the scene unfolds with a terrible clarity. For an instant, time is frozen. Your thoughts and sensory impressions are fragmented, each one stabbing at you like a needle.

The warden is at his post. So is the executioner and the attending physician. On the opposite side of the chamber, behind a guard rail less than four feet from where you sit, stand the official witnesses, their eyes riveted on you through the thick glass. In a matter of minutes, you'll be dead. They're here to watch you die.

The executioner is signaled by the warden. With scientific precision, valves are opened. Closed. Sodium cyanide eggs are dropped into the immersion pan—filled with sulphuric acid—beneath your metal chair. Up rise the deadly fumes. The cell is filled with the odor of bitter almond and peach blossoms. It's a sickening-sweet smell.

Only seconds of consciousness remain.

You inhale the deadly fumes. You become giddy. You strain against the straps as the blackness closes in. You exhale, inhale again. Your head aches.

There's a pain in your chest. But the ache, the pain is nothing. You're hardly aware of it. You're slipping into unconsciousness. You're dying. Your head jerks back. Only for an awful instant do you float free. Your brain has been denied oxygen. Your body fights a losing ten-minute battle against death.

You've stopped breathing. Your heart has quit beating.

You're dead.

The minutes pass. The blowers whirr. The ammonia valves are open. The gas is being driven from the cell. The clerical work is being done.

That's your body they're removing; it's your body they take to the prison morgue. No, don't worry about that cyanide rash on your leg.

If you have no one to claim your body and you're not of the Jewish or Catholic faith, you'll be shipped off to be cremated. You'll come back to the prison in a 'jar.' You'll go to Boot Hill.

> If your body is claimed, a mortician will come for it. He'll take you away to a funeral parlor, prepare you for burial, impersonally. Services? Well, that's up to your people. Then burial. The end. But not really the end.
>
> An aged mother may be weeping silently. She carried you in her womb. She gave you birth. And your life came to this.
>
> "Mommy," a little girl may ask, "where's Daddy?"
>
> Cruelly, a playmate may tell a small son, "Your old man died in the gas chamber!"
>
> A young wife is dazed, numb.
>
> This is your legacy to them.

Chessman had seen the execution process at work when many of his fellow condemned were taken to their deaths. He coped with the threat of his own execution, according to a psychiatrist who interviewed him on a number of occasions, "by thinking of himself as the attorney in the case rather than as the condemned man." When this stratagem failed, as it did periodically, Chessman would talk with his psychiatrist "about the feelings of torture that he experienced waiting for death. At times, he felt that he could no longer tolerate the pain, the anxiety, and the fear. At such times, he expressed a wish to get the suffering over with." Chessman never dropped his appeals, but his appeals did finally run out. After twelve years on death row, Chessman took his last walk.

"The death penalty is utterly out of step with our current standards of decency and has no place in our justice system."

As Chessman's fictional account implies . . . executioner and condemned alike are dehumanized in today's executions. They are morally dead—dead as persons—even as their bodies move to the cadence of this modern dance macabre. Each participates in a peculiarly subtle and insidious form of torture that prepares them for their respective roles in the execution process. This is not justice but rather, in Albert Camus's wise reckoning, administrative murder. To be sure, these arrangements make executions easier and more palatable. Indeed, given our modern sensibilities, there may well be no other way we can execute a person. But at bottom these dehumanizing procedures hide a reality that we must face head on—namely, that the death penalty is utterly out of step with our current standards of decency and has no place in our justice system.

Capital Punishment Undermines the Sacredness of Life

by the Permanent Deacons of Paterson, New Jersey

About the authors: *The Permanent Deacons of Paterson, New Jersey, are a group of 147 clergymen who preside over the Roman Catholic diocese of Paterson. The following viewpoint is a statement signed by all but eight of the active deacons.*

We, the deacons of the Diocese of Paterson, N.J., wish to address the faithful of our church and people of good will throughout the state of New Jersey regarding the question of capital punishment.

The ultimate punishment available to the state in the face of serious crime is the death penalty. Our position is rooted in our belief that human life is sacred and that we have an obligation to protect it and enhance it at all stages of development. Made in God's image and likeness, each person is the clearest reflection of the Creator and possesses a dignity that no one can take away.

A truly human and responsible society cannot abdicate its moral responsibilities regarding the many issues related to the protection and enhancement of human life. Because life is both sacred and social, society must protect and foster it at all stages and in all circumstances through institutions such as state government. When any human being becomes a victim of violence, we all suffer diminishment of our own human dignity. When any human life ends at the hands of another person, all human life becomes vulnerable.

Capital Punishment Is No Remedy

Capital punishment seeks to remedy violent crime or murder by taking the perpetrator's life. We are convinced, however, that this is not an appropriate response. We believe that capital punishment undermines rather than witnesses to the sacredness of human life. Moreover, capital punishment fails to effectively

Reprinted, with permission, from "The Problem with the Death Penalty," by the Permanent Deacons of Paterson, New Jersey, *Origins*, January 21, 1999.

combat crime and to build a society that is free from crime. Furthermore, capital punishment does not help relieve the pain and loss of the victims or their families.

Therefore, the undersigned deacons of the Roman Catholic Diocese of Paterson, N.J., are unalterably opposed to the death penalty.

As deacons, we are keenly aware of the experience of our people. With them we fear the continual increase of violent crime in our society. Innocent victims who survive, as well as victims' families and friends, suffer ongoing trauma because of the violence inflicted upon them and their loved ones.

"Capital punishment undermines rather than witnesses to the sacredness of human life."

Frequently little or no attention is given to the plight of victims. There is a need to examine proposals that seek to provide support, compensation and healing for victims and their families.

We and our fellow clergy have shared their pain and anxiety. We have buried the victims, have counseled their families and have undertaken a variety of efforts to prevent violence and promote reconciliation and healing. In contrast, death penalty cases generally cause healing to be delayed, if not made almost impossible. The death penalty does not allow the opportunity for the spiritual and human reconciliation with victim, survivors, perpetrator and God.

Violent crime forces society to invest substantial resources—sorely needed elsewhere—to identify, arrest, try, convict, sentence and incarcerate perpetrators. It is incumbent upon the state to address the root causes of crime or we will all suffer the consequences of living in a society overwhelmed by the demands of our criminal-justice system.

We cite a recent teaching of the U.S. Catholic bishops on violence: "Increasingly, our society looks to violent measures to deal with some of our most difficult social problems . . . including increased reliance on the death penalty to deal with crime. . . . Violence is not the solution: It is the most clear sign of our failures. . . . We cannot teach that killing is wrong by killing."

Why Capital Punishment Is Wrong

As citizens of New Jersey, we believe that the state must protect the people and discipline those who commit serious crimes against them. The question is how best to do this. In recent years many thoughtful people have concluded that capital punishment is not the answer:

- The death penalty does not effectively deter serious crime in our nation.
- The death penalty does not alleviate the fear of violent crime or better safeguard the people.
- The death penalty does not protect society more effectively than other alternatives such as life imprisonment without parole.
- The death penalty does not restore the social order breached by offenders.
- The death penalty is not imposed with fairness, falling disproportionately on

racial and ethnic minorities and the poor.

- The death penalty is not imposed in such a way as to prevent the execution of innocent death-row inmates.

Traditional Catholic teaching has allowed the taking of human life in particular circumstances by way of exception as, for example, in self-defense and capital punishment. Recently, however, the presumptions against taking human life through capital punishment [have] been strengthened and the exceptions made ever more restrictive.

Modern science and technology have allowed us to probe more deeply than ever into the very mystery of life. Such advances challenge us to a greater sensitivity to the questions of life and death. We have the obligation to use our knowledge for the enhancement of human life. We also have the responsibility to foster an attitude in the broader society which affirms this option for life. Moreover, it seems that the greater challenge is to apply this value to diverse issues in a consistent manner. While these various life issues are different and require separate analysis, a consistent ethic of life strongly suggests that capital punishment is not an appropriate response to crime in our land.

Justice Is Not Achieved Through Vengeance

While not denying the traditional position that the state has the right to employ capital punishment, many Catholic bishops, together with Popes Paul VI and John Paul II, have spoken against the exercise of that right by the state. The Catechism of the Catholic Church states that the death penalty is permissible in cases of "extreme gravity." However, "if bloodless means are sufficient to defend human lives against an aggressor and to protect public order and the safety of persons, public authority must limit itself to such means."

> ***"The death penalty does not allow the opportunity for the spiritual and human reconciliation with victim, survivors, perpetrator and God."***

Since publication of the Catechism of the Catholic Church, Pope John Paul II has clarified the teaching further for his global audience. In the strongest papal denunciation of the death penalty, he wrote in his encyclical *Evangelium Vitae* (1995):

> The nature and extent of the punishment must be carefully evaluated and decided upon, and ought not go to the extreme of executing the offender except in cases of absolute necessity: in other words, when it would not be possible otherwise to defend society. Today, however, as a result of steady improvements in the organization of the penal system, such cases are very rare, if not practically nonexistent.

We join our voices to his, arguing that more humane and effective methods of defending society exist and should be used.

Much of the support for the death penalty stems from a desire for revenge or to balance somehow the terrible damage that has been done. Such feelings may be expected in the face of brutal and senseless violence, especially when it has been inflicted upon innocent people. People legitimately desire justice. However, justice cannot be achieved through vengeance. "'Vengeance is mine, I will repay, says the Lord.'. . . Do not be conquered by evil, but conquer evil with good" (Rom. 12:19–21).

"We cannot teach that killing is wrong by killing."

Vengeance is never a worthy human motive. Our Scriptures direct us to a different ethic. The often-quoted proverb, "An eye for an eye, a tooth for a tooth" (Lv. 24:20), was not a prescription for revenge or a goad to further bloodshed, but a guideline to keep people from going beyond the original offense and escalating the violence. Jesus further clarified this position when he insisted that rather than retaliate on any level, we should offer the other cheek and extend our hand in blessing and healing (Mt. 5:38–48).

Fighting violence with violence does not achieve a useful purpose in society. Nor does it allow us to foster an ethic of respect of life that moves beyond vengeance in order to deal with violence in a more effective way.

To take a human life, even that of someone who is guilty, is awesome and tragic. It seems to us that in our culture today there are not sufficient reasons to justify the state to exercise its right in the matter of capital punishment. There are other, more effective ways of protecting the interests of society.

As citizens we share a common concern for the quality of life in our state. As ordained clergy ministering to our brothers and sisters we appreciate the moral and human dimensions of this difficult question.

Crime is both a manifestation of the great mysteries of evil and human freedom, and an aspect of the very complex reality that is contemporary society. We should not expect simple or easy solutions to what is a profound evil, and even less should we rely on capital punishment to provide such a solution.

Despite the opposition expressed by the U.S. bishops to the death penalty, we are aware that public opinion, including that of many Catholics, has widely supported it.

It is our purpose to build a broad-based consensus for a consistent ethic of life that recognizes the sanctity of every human being and seeks solutions to the problems of violence. This ethic of life truly serves the common good and does not further erode respect for life.

We, the undersigned deacons of the Roman Catholic Diocese of Paterson, N.J., are unalterably opposed to the death penalty. We encourage people of good will to reflect seriously and in an informed way on this important moral issue.

Chapter 2

Is Capital Punishment Administered Fairly?

The Death Penalty and Fairness: An Overview

by Mary H. Cooper

About the author: *Mary H. Cooper is a staff writer for* CQ Researcher, *a weekly report on current issues.*

It has been more than three years since Rolando Cruz was cleared of the charges that landed him on death row, but there's still bitterness in his voice. "I did 12 years, three months and three days," he told a recent conference on capital punishment. "They did kill me. I am who I am now because this is who they made."

Cruz and another man, Alejandro Hernandez, were sentenced to death for the 1983 abduction, rape and murder of 10-year-old Jeanine Nicarico of Naperville, Ill. It was the kind of high-profile crime that prompts communities to demand quick action by law enforcement officers. DuPage County authorities complied by charging Cruz and Hernandez with Jeanine's murder.

Both men were tried, convicted and sentenced to death in 1985. Their convictions were based largely on the testimony of jailhouse informants and a deputy sheriff who said Cruz's description of a dream included details about the murder that only the killer would have known.

In 1995, after more than 10 years on death row, Cruz and Hernandez were released from prison after DNA testing proved that another man had raped Jeanine. At the time of the murder, Brian Dugan, a repeat sex offender and confessed murderer, had told authorities that he alone had committed the crime—a fact that the Cruz and Hernandez juries weren't told. Three prosecutors and four law enforcement officers have since been charged with obstruction of justice for concealing evidence that would have exonerated the men a decade earlier.

Wrongful Convictions

The Cruz and Hernandez cases may be dramatic, but they're hardly unique. Five hundred people have been executed in the United States since the Supreme Court reinstated the death penalty in 1976. Over that same period, 75 con-

Excerpted from "Death Penalty Update," by Mary H. Cooper, *CQ Researcher*, January 8, 1999. Reprinted with permission.

demned inmates have been released after evidence showed they had been wrongfully convicted. That equates to roughly one exoneration for every seven executions.

"If you had to go to a hospital for a life-and-death operation and found that hospital misdiagnosed [one out of every seven] cases, you'd run," said lawyer Barry Scheck, a member of O.J. Simpson's defense team. "It's an intolerable level of error, regardless of your views on the death penalty."

"Recent studies have documented longstanding allegations of racial discrimination in capital cases."

Scheck spoke at a 1998 national conference on wrongful conviction and the death penalty at Northwestern University Law School. "We don't have a position on the ultimate morality of the death penalty," says conference participant Richard C. Dieter, executive director of the Death Penalty Information Center in Washington. "It's how the death penalty is applied in the United States that we are critical of. We say that there's a lot of unfairness and that mistakes are made, and that at least we should attempt to change and correct those things."

Indeed, no one is predicting the death penalty will be abolished anytime soon in the United States. Capital punishment is on the books in 38 states, plus the federal government and the military. There are now 3,517 prisoners around the country awaiting execution.

A large majority of Americans still support capital punishment, and that support seems unlikely to wane in the wake of several horrific crimes in the past few years. Few protested the death sentence meted out to an unrepentant Timothy J. McVeigh for his role in the 1995 bombing of the Alfred P. Murrah Federal Building in Oklahoma City, which killed 168 people. And many Americans were angered when Susan Smith was sentenced in South Carolina to life in prison rather than death after drowning her two young children in 1994 and charging a mysterious black man with the crime. Similarly, many thought "Unabomber" Theodore Kaczynski deserved the death penalty for mailing letter bombs that left three people dead and 22 others injured.

Is the System Fair?

Death penalty advocates say leniency in some of these cases shows that the system works by sparing mentally ill or mentally retarded criminals. But many legal experts point to flaws in the death penalty's application that open the criminal justice system to charges of pervasive unfairness. Recent studies have documented longstanding allegations of racial discrimination in capital cases. Statistics show that prisoners of all races are more likely to be executed if the victim was white than some other race. Although about half the homicide victims are people of color, more than 80 percent of the prisoners executed were convicted of killing whites. A 1998 study also suggests that blacks are the most likely to receive the death penalty, regardless of the victim's race.

"These studies are trying to determine whether race discrimination accounts for the race disparities in sentencing," says Dieter, author of the [1998] study. "The odds of getting the death penalty are much higher if you're black than if you're white."

Defenders of capital punishment counter that any racial discrimination that may exist in its application argues for expanding the use of capital punishment, not abolishing it. "If it is true that people who kill black victims are less likely to get sentenced to death, that doesn't show the death penalty is discriminatorily imposed," says Kent S. Scheidegger, legal director at the Criminal Justice Legal Foundation in Sacramento, Calif. "It shows the death penalty is discriminatorily withheld. And the answer to that is more death sentences, not fewer, for the same kinds of crime in black-victim cases."

Another area of concern has been the death penalty's application to mentally retarded or mentally ill prisoners. The U.S. Supreme Court ruled in 1986 that the Eighth Amendment prohibits the execution of insane prisoners, but the definition of insanity varies widely among jurisdictions. Although evidence of mental illness led courts to spare Kaczynski and Smith, many less notorious killers have been executed despite evidence that they were unable to discern the seriousness of their crimes. In fact, 12 mentally retarded people have been executed since 1976; only 12 states prohibit the death penalty for the mentally retarded.

Much of the current criticism of capital punishment concerns recently implemented restrictions on habeas corpus, a procedure for challenging a state conviction or sentence in federal court on constitutional grounds after normal appeals have been exhausted. The Constitution enshrines this right in Article 1, Section 9, and forbids the suspension of habeas corpus except in cases involving rebellion or invasion that threaten the public safety.

The mounting crime rates of the late 1980s prompted Congress to pass the 1996 Anti-Terrorism and Effective Death Penalty Act. Among other things, the sweeping measure not only set a one-year deadline for submitting a habeas corpus petition after state appeals are exhausted but also limited prisoners to one appeal in most cases. Supporters of the measure wanted to deter prisoners from launching repeated and groundless petitions to stall their executions.

Critics say the 1996 law fails to recognize the importance of the appeals process, compounding the unfairness of capital punishment. Most defendants in capital cases cannot afford experienced defense attorneys, and many don't receive adequate counsel, critics say, either at trial or during the appeals process.

In 1997, the American Bar Association (ABA) called for a moratorium on executions, citing "a haphazard maze of unfair practices with no internal consistency." But public support for the death penalty continues to run high, making the prospects doubtful for substantive reform in the near future.

Capital Punishment Is Applied Unfairly

by Jesse Jackson Sr. and Jesse Jackson Jr.

About the authors: *Jesse Jackson Sr. is president of the National Rainbow Coalition, a social justice organization. He has been active in civil rights issues since the 1960s. Jesse Jackson Jr. is a Democratic congressman from Illinois.*

Who receives the death penalty has less to do with the violence of the crime than with the color of the criminal's skin or, more often, the color of the victim's skin. Murder—always tragic—seems to be a more heinous and despicable crime in some states than in others. Women who kill and who are killed are judged by different standards than are men who are murderers and victims.

The death penalty is essentially an arbitrary punishment. There are no objective rules or guidelines for when a prosecutor should seek the death penalty, when a jury should recommend it, and when a judge should give it. This lack of objective, measurable standards ensures that the application of the death penalty will be discriminatory against racial, gender, and ethnic groups.

The majority of Americans who support the death penalty believe, or wish to believe, that legitimate factors such as the violence and cruelty with which the crime was committed, a defendant's culpability or history of violence, and the number of victims involved determine who is sentenced to life in prison and who receives the ultimate punishment. The numbers, however, tell a different story. They confirm the terrible truth that bias and discrimination warp our nation's judicial system at the very time it matters most—in matters of life and death. The factors that determine who will live and who will die—race, sex, and geography—are the very same ones that blind justice was meant to ignore. This prejudicial distribution should be a moral outrage to every American.

The Where and How of Executions

On September 1, 1995, legislation reinstituting the death penalty went into effect in New York, bringing the total number of states with the death penalty to 38. Sadly, the list of states that do not employ capital punishment seems woefully short: Alaska, Hawaii, Iowa, Maine, Massachusetts, Michigan, Minnesota, North Dakota, Rhode Island, Vermont, West Virginia, Wisconsin, and the District of Columbia remain the only jurisdictions that have not adopted legal murder.

Between 1976, when the Supreme Court reinstated the use of capital punishment, and June 1996, 330 death row inmates have been executed. Over that period, the number of executions per year has generally risen. After a slow start—there were no executions in 1976 and only one in 1977—the rate started rising rapidly. Every year since 1984, the number of condemned prisoners executed has been in the double digits. With concerted efforts in the states and in Congress to cut off death row appeals, it appears that each new year will see a new record for executions.

The methods used and frequency of executions vary widely from state to state. Far and away the most popular methods are lethal injection, authorized by 32 states and used in 193 executions; and electrocution, legal in 11 states and used in 123 executions. A distant third is the gas chamber, an option in seven states and used in nine executions. Although we deceive ourselves if we believe there are humane ways to take life, it seems particularly barbaric that four states authorize hanging and have carried out three executions in this manner; and that two states, Idaho and Utah, sanction execution by firing squad, with two executions having been performed this way.

Geography and the Death Penalty

Murders committed in certain regions of our country are much more likely to result in the death penalty than are murders in other regions. The southern states (Alabama, Arkansas, Florida, Georgia, Louisiana, Mississippi, North Carolina, Oklahoma, South Carolina, Texas, Virginia) are host to a disproportionate percentage of executions. Home to roughly 26 percent of our nation's population, these states have carried out 83 percent of our nation's executions since 1976. If you commit murder in a southern state, you are roughly three times more likely to be executed for the crime there as elsewhere. In contrast, the northeastern states have a much larger population, generally lower murder rates, and accounted for only two executions (both in Pennsylvania), or less than 1 percent of the executions since 1976.

Texas—which accounts for little more than 6 percent of the nation's population—has executed 106 death row inmates, or a staggering 32 percent of the national total. Despite this liberal use of the death penalty, the state's murder rate is 25 percent higher than the national average—in 1992, 12.7 per 100,000 compared to 9.3 per 100,000 nationwide.

Thus, after 20 years of the highest rate of execution in the country, Texas continues to outpace the rest of the country in its rate of murder. This explodes the myth of capital punishment being an effective deterrent. It also gives us a glimpse of how unevenly and in many cases prejudicially capital punishment is applied.

Race and the Death Penalty

The relationship between race and capital punishment is much more complex than most people suppose. One surprise for many people is that more white defendants than black defendants have been executed. Since 1976, according to the Death Penalty Information Center, 56 percent of the condemned prisoners executed have been white, 38 percent have been black, and 6 percent have been Hispanic, Native American, or Asian. And death row population statistics reflect similar percentages. As of January 1996, 48 percent of the inmates on death row were white, 41 percent were black, 7.5 percent were Hispanic, and 3.5 percent were listed as "other."

These statistics are simply the beginning of a chain that is not generally reported by the media, and so is not known by the public. Numerous researchers have shown conclusively that African American defendants are far more likely to receive the death penalty than are white defendants charged with the same crime. For instance, African Americans make up 25 percent of Alabama's population, yet of Alabama's 117 death row inmates, 43 percent are black. Indeed, 71 percent of the people executed there since the resumption of capital punishment have been black.

The population of Georgia's Middle Judicial Circuit is 40 percent black, but 77 percent of the circuit's capital decisions have been found against black defendants. The Ocmulgee Judicial Circuit posts remarkably similar numbers. In 79 percent of the cases in which the district attorney sought the death penalty, the defendant was black, despite the fact that only 44 percent of the circuit's population is black. More ominously, in the cases where black defendants faced capital prosecution, 90 percent of the district attorney's peremptory strikes were used to keep African Americans off the juries.

> ***"The application of the death penalty [is] discriminatory against racial, gender, and ethnic groups."***

And this disproportion in capital sentencing is not just a Southern problem, for the results of the 1988 federal law providing for a death penalty for drug kingpins are telling. In 1993, all nine defendants approved for capital prosecution were African Americans. Of the first 36 cases in which prosecutors sought the death penalty under this new legislation, four of the defendants were white, four were Hispanic, and 28 were black.

The Victim's Race Is Influential

It is not just the race of the defendant that affects the state's decision of whether to seek the death penalty and whether it is meted out. The race of the victim—more specifically, whether or not the victim was white—can have an even stronger influence.

Dr. David Baldus of the University of Iowa has studied over 2,500 Georgia murder cases. Controlling for 230 nonracial factors in the cases, he found that defendants accused of murdering a white victim are 4.3 times more likely to receive the death penalty than defendants accused of killing blacks. Baldus determined that the race of the murderer was less important than the race of the victim. Fewer than 40 percent of the homicide victims in Georgia are white, yet fully 87 percent of the cases resulting in the death penalty involved white victims.

"African American defendants are far more likely to receive the death penalty than are white defendants charged with the same crime."

Baldus cited one judicial circuit in Georgia where, despite the fact that 65 percent of the homicide cases involved African American victims, 85 percent of the cases in which the district attorney sought the death penalty were against murderers of whites. Overall, this particular district attorney sought the death penalty in 34 percent of the cases involving white victims but a mere 5.8 percent of the cases in which the victim was black.

Georgia is not the only state where the color of the victim's skin can mean the difference between life and death. Nationwide, even though 50 percent of murder victims are African American, says the Death Penalty Information Center, almost 85 percent of the victims in death penalty cases are white. And in their 1989 book *Death and Discrimination*: *Racial Disparities in Capital Sentencing*, Samuel Gross and Robert Mauro analyzed sentencing in capital cases in Arkansas, Florida, Georgia, Illinois, Mississippi, North Carolina, Oklahoma, and Virginia during a period when these states accounted for 379 of the 1,011 death penalties nationwide. They found widespread discrepancies in sentencing based on the *victim's* race in all eight states.

Defendants in Florida, for example, who killed whites received the death penalty eight times more often than those defendants convicted of killing African Americans. In Bay County, blacks are the victims of 40 percent of the murders, yet in all 17 cases between 1975 and 1987 in which a death sentence was handed down, the victims were white.

As one study after another confirmed the correlation between the race of the homicide victim and whether the defendant would receive a capital sentence, the evidence became so overwhelming that Congress's General Accounting Office (GAO) decided to take up the question itself. In its February 1990 report *Death Penalty Sentencing*, the GAO reviewed 28 studies based on 23 sets of data and concluded, "In eighty-two percent of the studies, race of the victim was found to influence the likelihood of being charged with capital murder or receiving the death penalty, i.e., those who murdered whites were found more likely to be sentenced to death than those who murdered blacks."

And when a case involves interracial murder, the bias against black homicide defendants multiplies the effects of the bias against the murderers of white victims. Since 1976, only four white defendants have been executed for killing a black person, yet 75 black defendants have been executed for murdering a white person. Astoundingly, African Americans who murder whites are *19 times as likely to be executed* as whites who kill blacks.

In 1987, Warren McCleskey, a black man armed with formidable evidence linking the victim's race with the distribution of the death penalty, appealed to the Supreme Court to overturn his death sentence. He argued that the fact his victim was white played an important role in his sentencing. Although the Court acknowledged that the correlation of the victim's race and the imposition of the death penalty was "statistically significant in the system as a whole," it denied McCleskey's petition saying that the burden is on the defendant to prove his individual sentence was based on his victim's race. McCleskey was executed on September 25, 1991.

In response to the *McCleskey* decision, the Racial Justice Act was introduced in Congress in 1994. The purpose of the act was to allow condemned prisoners to appeal their death sentences using evidence of past discriminatory sentencing—the kind of evidence that failed to save McCleskey. After passing in the House 217–212, the bill failed in the Senate. To date, there has been no precedent set for citing biased sentencing patterns to successfully appeal a death sentence.

With black men nearly eight times more likely to be victims of homicide than white men, could there be a more blatant message from the criminal justice system that it values some lives more highly than others? Not in a loud voice that would attract undue attention, but quietly and methodically, one prosecution at a time, our judicial system is telling us that African American life is less important than white life, and its annihilation less tragic. Our judicial system is demonstrably, institutionally racist in the end result, and the end result—killing a disproportionate number of black males—matters.

Gender and the Death Penalty

North Carolina prison officials described Velma Barfield as a model prisoner. She read the Bible daily and offered support and counsel to younger inmates. Properly diagnosed and treated, the bipolar behavior that had plagued Barfield was under control, and she was making a life for herself in prison.

But Velma Barfield was a condemned woman. In 1978, she was convicted of murdering her fiancé, Stuart Taylor, and confessed to the arsenic poisonings of three others, including her mother. She received the death penalty for her crime. Six years later, on November 2, 1984, after numerous appeals to delay her execution failed, her time had come.

In her final words, she expressed her remorse. "I want to say that I am sorry for all the hurt that I have caused. I know that everybody has gone through a lot of pain, all the families connected, and I am sorry, and I want to thank everybody who has supported me all these six years." After a last meal of cola and cheese puffs, Barfield was dressed in a pair of pink pajamas and was strapped onto a gurney and given a sleep-inducing drug. Fifteen minutes after North Carolina prison officials administered a lethal dose of procuronium bromide, this 52-year-old grandmother became the first woman executed since the Supreme Court reinstated the death penalty in 1976. . . .

That few women have been executed in the last 20 years has prompted more than one legal scholar to suggest that female homicide defendants benefit from preferential discrimination. The most notable critic has been the late Justice Thurgood Marshall who, in his concurring opinion in *Furman v. Georgia,* rhetorically asked what other explanation could be given for the discrepancy between the number of women who commit murder and the much smaller number who receive the death penalty.

> ***"African Americans who murder whites are* 19 times as likely to be executed *as whites who kill blacks."***

Data in the FBI's Supplementary Homicide Reports state that about 14 percent of all known murder and non-negligent manslaughter suspects are women. However, as of January 1996, only 1.6 percent of the inmates on death row are women, according to *Death Row, U.S.A.*

Elizabeth Rapaport is one of the few researchers studying gender and the death penalty. She cites two legitimate factors that influence women's lower rate of capital punishment: prior criminal record and seriousness of the offense (the violence and brutality with which the murder was committed). Prior conviction for a violent felony is one factor that may lead a prosecutor to seek a capital trial. Twenty percent of male defendants have a history of violent felony convictions, whereas only 4 percent of female defendants have such a history. Women are also substantially less likely to commit murders with excessive force and brutality or with multiple victims.

Rapaport estimates that if men and women were judged equally—i.e., if only the circumstances that should legitimately influence the prosecution and sentencing in a case, such as prior record and excessive cruelty, were considered—we should expect about 4 percent of death row inmates to be women. The difference between that figure and the current percentage of women on death row suggests that women accused of murder may be as much as two-and-a-half times less likely to face capital punishment because of their gender.

Other evidence points to another twist in the tale of capital punishment. It appears that a woman's relationship to her victim may influence the punishment she receives, just as the race of the victim does.

Overall, homicide defendants are much more likely to receive the death penalty for the murder of strangers for economic gain than they are for the murder of intimate family members—including children—in anger. Once again, the gravity of the crime seems to depend upon the identity of its victim. (Eighty percent of the victims of predatory murder are men, while women are six times more likely than men to be murdered by an intimate.)

However, the statistical tables are turned concerning women who take the life of a spouse or a close family member. Women who kill those who are close to them are more likely to receive the ultimate penalty than men who kill those close to them. In North Carolina, for example, a man who kills a stranger is twice as likely to receive the death penalty as a man who kills an intimate or a family member. But the percentage of women on death row who have killed intimates much more closely resembles the rate at which women kill those close to them: 65 percent of the murders women commit are against intimates, and 49 percent of the women on death row killed spouses or family members. Surely, it seems that our society's continued assignment to women of the roles of nurturers and keepers of the family that influences our judicial system to deem women's murdering of family members as somehow more reprehensible—or more dangerous—than the same offenses committed by men.

My goal is not to question whether killing a loved one or a stranger is the more heinous crime. Taking any life is a terrible matter. Nor do I wish to suggest that more women should be executed for the murders they commit. Rather, my purpose is to point out that women who kill are held to different standards than are men who kill. Whether these standards are prejudicial for them or against them, the point is that they *are* different. Gender joins race and geography as another factor by which the death penalty is inflicted differentially and prejudicially.

We are confronted with the undeniable evidence that the death penalty is handed down unjustly. The reaction of most state governments to this evidence has been to assert that the death penalty is still necessary, and that what is needed is a way of ensuring that it is distributed fairly and handed down for the right reasons. At this time, the Supreme Court agrees with the majority of the states. The goal of implementing a fair system for imposing the death penalty, however, has proved very elusive. And the statistics that are proving the failure of this policy have been produced under the supposedly stricter post-*Furman* laws.

Thirty-five years in the civil rights struggle has taught me that you can't legislate acceptance, objectivity, or morality. How then, at the moment between life and death, is society to erase a lifetime of social conditioning, assumptions, and attitudes the judges and jurors may not even realize they hold? There is no way the states, the federal government, or the judicial system can ensure that every prosecuting attorney, every jury member, and every judge involved in every homicide case is impartial and unbiased. And in the case of the death penalty, the stakes are just too high for even one life to be lost to prejudice and hatred.

"Women who kill those who are close to them are more likely to receive the ultimate penalty than men who kill those close to them."

Racism Influences Death-Sentence Decisions

by Michael B. Ross

About the author: *Michael B. Ross has been on Connecticut's death row since June of 1987. He is currently under a stay of execution pending resolution of the appeals process.*

"The evidence shows that there is a better than even chance in Georgia that race will influence the decision to impose the death penalty: a majority of defendants in white-victim crimes would not have been sentenced to die if their victims had been black."

Surprisingly, those words were written by former U.S. Supreme Court Justice William Brennan when he criticized the Court majority for continuing to uphold a "capital-sentencing system in which race more likely than not plays a role. . . ."

Racism: it's a nasty word, and many people would prefer to look the other way and deny its existence. But not only does it exist, it exists in one of the most sensitive areas of our judicial system—capital punishment.

The question of racial discrimination in capital sentencing procedures has prompted an ongoing debate. Retired U.S. Supreme Court Justice Harry Blackmun deplored our country's continued use of the death penalty, stating: "I feel morally and intellectually obligated simply to concede that the death penalty experiment has failed." He further stated, "It surely is beyond dispute that if the death penalty cannot be administered consistently and rationally, it may not be administered at all."

There is much evidence to show that race is an important factor in determining who will be sentenced to die for a crime and who will receive a lesser punishment for the same crime. Extensive research on capital sentencing patterns over the past two decades has repeatedly found that racism, whether conscious or subconscious, permeates decisions of life and death in both state and federal courts throughout the United States.

Reprinted, with permission, from "The Death Penalty in Black and White," by Michael B. Ross, *Friends Journal*, June 1996.

The Racial Makeup of Death Row

One simple way to see this is to examine the makeup of the current death row population. According to the NAACP's [National Association for the Advancement of Colored People] Legal Defense and Education Fund publication, "Death Row, U.S.A.," as of August 31, 1995, 1,224 (40%) of prisoners under sentence of death in the U.S. were black, despite the fact that blacks compose only about 12% of the national population. In some states, blacks condemned to death outnumber whites condemned to death. Finally, if you consider all minorities as a group, 1,561 (52%) of the 3,028 men and women on death row today are non-white.

Consider a few figures from the August 31, 1995, issue of "Death Row, U.S.A.":

Mississippi—35 (63%) of their 56 death row inmates are black; blacks make up 36% of the state's population.

North Carolina—71 (47%) of their 151 death row inmates are black; blacks make up 23% of the state's population.

Virginia—27 (49%) of their 55 death row inmates are black; blacks make up 19% of the state's population.

Although many people find these statistics shocking, others might not be surprised. After all, the South has always been perceived as being more racist than the rest of the country. Consider a few figures from some other, non-Southern states:

Illinois—100 (62%) of their 161 death row inmates are black; blacks make up 25% of the state's population.

Ohio—73 (50%) of their 146 death row inmates are black; blacks make up 10% of the state's population.

Pennsylvania—118 (61%) of their 193 death row inmates are black; blacks make up 10% of the state's population.

Killers of Whites Are More Likely to Receive the Death Penalty

Statistics on the race of offenders do not necessarily prove bias given that roughly 50 percent of those arrested for murder are black. Of far more significance are the racial disparities revealed by an examination of the race of murder *victims* in cases where the death penalty is imposed. Numerous studies have been conducted to try to quantify the extent of racial disparities in capital cases. One study done in the late 1970s at Northeastern University in Boston, Mass., by William Bowers and Glenn Pierce compared statistics on all criminal homicides and death sentences imposed in Florida, Georgia, Texas, and Ohio. Death sentences in those four states accounted for 70% of all death sentences imposed nationally at that time. They found that although most killers of whites were white, blacks who killed whites were proportionately more likely to receive the death sentence than any other group.

In Florida and Texas, for example, blacks who killed whites were, respectively, five and six times more likely to be sentenced to death than whites who killed whites. Among black offenders in Florida, those who killed whites were 40 times more likely to get the death penalty than those who killed blacks. No white offender in Florida had ever been sentenced to death for the killing of a black up through the period studied. (A white man sentenced to death in Florida in 1980 for killing a black woman was the first white person in the state to be sentenced to death for the murder of a sole black person—and he has yet to be executed).

Several other studies, conducted in a variety of capital punishment states, have arrived at the same conclusion: killers of whites are far more likely to be sentenced to death than killers of blacks.

Northeastern University published a study conducted in the early 1980s by David Baldus that sought to discover why killers of white victims in Georgia received the death penalty approximately 11 times more often than killers of black victims.

Baldus found that the two most significant points affecting the likelihood of a death sentence were the prosecutor's decisions on whether or not to permit a plea bargain and whether or not to seek a death sentence after a murder conviction. Black-victim murder convictions were far more likely to result in pleas to manslaughter or life sentences than cases with white victims. Black defendants with white victims were less likely than others to have their charges reduced and more likely than others, upon conviction of murder, to receive the death penalty.

> ***"Racism, whether conscious or subconscious, permeates decisions of life and death in both state and federal courts throughout the United States."***

Baldus noted that the prosecutors had sought the death penalty in only 40% of the cases where defendants were convicted of capital crimes; the others received automatic life sentences without a penalty hearing. Perhaps the most disturbing finding was that although cases with white victims tended to be more aggravated in general, the levels of aggravation in crimes involving black victims had to be substantially higher before prosecutors would seek the death penalty. Thus the overall disparities in death sentencing were due more to the prosecutor's charging and sentencing decisions than to any jury sentencing decisions.

Other Racial Disparities in Sentencing

Several other studies have also found significant racial disparities in prosecutors' decisions on charging. The Bowers study found that the victim's race had a significant "extra-legal" influence on whether or not a capital charge would be filed. A study done by Michael Radelet and Glenn Pierce, "Race and Prosecutorial Discretion in Homicide Cases," found a tendency by prosecutors to "upgrade" cases with white victims and "downgrade" those with black victims.

These findings do not necessarily imply that prosecutors deliberately discriminate in their charging and sentencing decisions. In areas with a large white majority population that strongly supports the use of capital punishment, there is inevitably more pressure on prosecutors to seek a death sentence in cases with white victims than there is in those with black victims or other minorities. Also, in general, there is more community outrage, publicity, and public pressure when the murder victim comes from a middle-class background, which is unfortunately more likely to apply to whites than to blacks.

> ***"Blacks who [kill] whites [are] proportionately more likely to receive the death sentence than any other group."***

The issue was well summed up in "Patterns of Death: An Analysis of Racial Disparities in Capital Sentencing and Homicide Victimization" by Gross and Mauro:

> Since death penalty prosecutions require large allocations of scarce prosecutorial resources, prosecutors must choose a small number of cases to receive this expensive treatment. In making these choices they may favor homicides that are visible and disturbing to the community, and these will tend to be white-victim homicides.

In 1987 the U.S. Supreme Court examined the issue of racial discrimination in the death penalty in the case of *McCleskey v. Kemp,* to determine if Georgia's capital punishment system violated the Equal Protection Clause of the 14th Amendment. The Court demanded a seemingly impossible (and for many observers, a clearly unfair) level of proof, for the defendant was required to prove either that the decision-makers in his particular case had acted with a discriminatory intent or purpose or that the Georgia State Legislature had enacted or maintained the death penalty statute because of an anticipated racially discriminatory effect.

The Court, by a narrow five to four majority, concluded that statistics alone do not prove that race entered into any capital sentencing decision in any one particular case. The Court further noted that:

> Any mode for determining guilt or punishment has its weaknesses and potential for misuse. Despite such imperfections, constitutional guarantees are met when the mode for determining guilt or punishment has been surrounded with safeguards to make it as fair as possible.

The majority indicated that the arguments should be presented to the individual state legislative bodies, for it is their responsibility, not the Court's, to determine the appropriate punishment for particular crimes. They noted that:

> Despite McCleskey's wide-ranging arguments that basically challenge the validity of capital punishment in our multiracial society, the only question before us is whether in his case . . . the law of Georgia was properly applied.

In a dissenting opinion, Justice John Paul Stevens noted:

> The Court's decision appears to be based on a fear that acceptance of McCleskey's claim would sound the death knell for capital punishment. . . . If

> society were indeed forced to choose between a racially discriminatory death penalty (one that provides heightened protection "for whites only") and no death penalty at all, the choice mandated by the Constitution would be plain.

It is interesting to note that two of the justices who voted with the majority in 1987 now believe that they made the wrong decision. Both former Justices Lewis Powell and Harry Blackmun have stated they should have voted with the minority. That would have made the decision six to three in favor of McCleskey, which would have effectively outlawed capital punishment as racially biased in violation of the Equal Protection Clause of the 14th Amendment of the U.S. Constitution.

Following the McCleskey ruling, a Congressional bill entitled the "Racial Justice Act" was drafted. The bill would forbid "racially disproportionate capital sentencing" and would outlaw any death sentence found to have been imposed in a racially discriminatory manner. The Racial Justice Act was debated and defeated in the U.S. Senate by a vote of 52 to 35 on October 13, 1988. In subsequent years, this same bill has been defeated on every occasion that it has come up for a vote.

Racism in the Judicial System Cannot Be Tolerated

We cannot continue to live with the illusion that capital punishment works in the perfect, unbiased manner that we desire. While we may wish otherwise, race has an indisputable and integral part in our capital punishment system. The overwhelming evidence is not speculative or theoretical but empirical. One of the most telling statistics from the Baldus study was that six of every eleven defendants convicted of killing a white person would not have received the death penalty if their victim had been black. These figures may vary from state to state, but the underlying conclusion remains the same: the taking of a white life is worth greater punishment than the taking of a black life. This is clearly unacceptable and can no longer be tolerated.

Justice Brennan once wrote: "We have demanded a uniquely high degree of rationality in imposing the death penalty. A capital sentencing system in which race more likely than not plays a role does not meet this standard."

> ***"We must do all we can to prevent race from being a factor in determining who lives and who dies for a given crime."***

Racism cannot be tolerated, especially in a punishment as final as capital punishment. It is clearly time to abolish the death penalty. It is no longer consistent with the values of our supposedly enlightened and humanistic society. We have evolved beyond the need for such a savage and barbaric punishment symbolic of our less-civilized past. There are suitable alternatives that are more humane and more consistent with our current values. The choice is not between the death penalty and unconditional release but between the death penalty and meaningful long-term sentences. The replacement of capital punishment with natural life sentences (with no possibility of release) is clearly a suitable alternative that fulfills society's requirements of protection. Race will undoubtedly still be a factor in other non-capital cases, until we can find a way for our society to resolve its problems with racial discrimination in the judicial system. We must do all we can to prevent race from being a factor in determining who lives and who dies for a given crime. It is the least we can do.

The Litigation Process for Capital Defendants Is Unfair

by Individual Rights and Responsibilities Death Penalty Committee

About the author: *The Individual Rights and Responsibilities Death Penalty Committee is an investigative arm of the American Bar Association.*

The federal Anti-Terrorism and Effective Death Penalty Act, enacted in 1996, includes provisions that severely undermine death row inmates' ability to use federal *habeas corpus* procedures to challenge their unconstitutional convictions or death sentences. [These procedures allow convicts to have their cases reviewed in a federal court.] Death row inmates have been subjected to numerous due process violations, particularly in state courts, in the litigation and appeal of capital punishment cases. The new limitations on the *habeas corpus* process likely will preclude the federal courts from considering many meritorious claims of due process violations.

In light of the fact that 40 percent of death row inmates' federal *habeas corpus* challenges have succeeded because state courts have failed to rectify due process violations in death penalty cases, and in light of the new significant restrictions on federal court review of such claims, an urgent situation exists in the litigation of capital cases.

The American Bar Association (ABA), as an organization of lawyers with particular expertise on due process and litigation issues, has an obligation to address the problem now. The urgency is all the greater because of Congress' complete defunding in 1996 of the post-conviction defender organizations that had mentored lawyers handling federal *habeas* cases and had handled many such cases themselves. The ABA has long supported the ABA Post-Conviction Death Penalty Representation Project, which has played a major role in the creation of these defender organizations. . . .

The Need for Decisive Action

The ABA has policies opposing the imposition of the death penalty on juveniles and persons with mental retardation; urging the appointment of experienced, competent and adequately compensated trial counsel during litigation of death penalty cases; and urging the adoption of Guidelines for the Appointment and Performance of Counsel in Death Penalty cases.

The ABA has policy urging greater fairness in federal *habeas corpus* proceedings, such as stays of execution during one full round of post-conviction litigation, consideration of claims not raised in state court because of the ignorance or neglect of counsel, and consideration of successive petitions that include claims undermining confidence in the prisoner's guilt or death sentence. . . .

The time has now come for the ABA to take additional decisive action with regard to capital punishment. Not only have the ABA's existing policies generally not been implemented, but also, and more critically, the federal and state governments have been moving in a direction contrary to these policies.

Of course, individual lawyers differ in their views on the death penalty in principle and on its constitutionality. However, it should now be apparent to all of us in the profession that the administration of the death penalty has become seriously flawed. The two recently enacted federal laws, together with other federal and state actions taken since the ABA adopted its policies on capital punishment, have resulted in a situation in which fundamental due process is now systematically lacking in capital cases. Accordingly, in order to effectuate its existing policies, the ABA should now call upon jurisdictions with capital punishment not to carry out the death penalty until these policies, or policies consistent with them, are implemented.

Competent Counsel

The ABA is especially well positioned to identify the professional legal services that should be available to capital defendants and death row inmates. The Association has conducted studies and adopted policies over 20 years ago.

In 1990, the ABA recommended that "competent and adequately compensated" counsel should be provided "at all stages of capital . . . litigation," including trial, direct review, collateral proceedings in both state and federal court, and certiorari proceedings in the U.S. Supreme Court. To implement that basic recommendation, the ABA said that death penalty jurisdictions should establish organizations to "recruit, select, train, monitor, support, and assist" attorneys representing capital clients.

In 1989, the ABA published the "Guidelines for the Appointment and Performance of Counsel in Death Penalty Cases" and urged all jurisdictions that employ the death penalty to adopt them. Those guidelines call for the appointment of two experienced attorneys at each stage of a capital case, by a special appointing authority or committee charged to identify and recruit lawyers with specified professional credentials, experience, and skills. The guidelines make it clear that ordinary professional qualifications are inadequate to measure what is needed from counsel in "the specialized practice of capital representation." To ensure that the lawyers assigned to capital cases are able to do the work required, the guidelines state that attorneys should receive a "reasonable rate of hourly compensation which . . . reflects the extraordinary responsibilities inherent in death penalty litigation." Concomitantly, counsel should be provided with the time and funding necessary for proper investigations, expert witnesses, and other support services.

No state has fully embraced the system the ABA has prescribed for capital trials. To the contrary, grossly unqualified and undercompensated lawyers who have nothing like the support necessary to mount an adequate defense are often appointed to represent capital clients. In case after case, decisions about who will die and who will live turn on the nature of the legal representation the defendant receives.

"The administration of the death penalty has become seriously flawed."

Most jurisdictions that employ the death penalty have proven unwilling to establish the kind of legal services system that is necessary to ensure that defendants charged with capital offenses receive the defense they require. Many death penalty states have no working public defender programs, relying instead upon scattershot methods for selecting and supporting defense counsel in capital cases. For example, some states simply assign lawyers at random from a general list—a scheme destined to identify attorneys who lack the necessary qualifications and, worse still, regard their assignments as a burden. Other jurisdictions employ "contract" systems, which typically channel indigent defense business to attorneys who offer the lowest bids. Other states use public defender schemes that appear on the surface to be more promising, but often prove in practice to be ineffective.

Poorly prepared and supported trial lawyers typically do a poor job. When they do recognize points to be explored and argued, they often fail to follow through in a professional manner. And when they do not recognize what needs to be done, they do nothing at all or they take actions that are inimical to the needs of their clients.

The result of such inadequacies in representation is that counsel often fail to present crucial facts. They also may fail to raise crucial legal issues, negligently causing their clients to forfeit their opportunity to explore those issues later—in any court. In one recent case, appointed defense counsel scarcely did anything to represent his client at trial and, along the way, neglected to raise three significant constitutional claims. The federal court that reviewed the case would not consider any of these omitted claims because, under state law, counsel's numerous defaults barred their later consideration.

The same pattern exists with respect to the legal services available for the appellate and post-conviction stages of capital cases. State appellate court standards for adequate representation under state law are extraordinarily low. These courts sometimes dispose of capital appeals on the basis of inadequate briefs containing only a few pages of argument; and they often rely on defense counsel's "default" at trial to avoid considering constitutional claims on the merits. As for post-conviction, an ABA Task Force developed an enormous body of evidence in 1990 demonstrating that prisoners sentenced to death typically receive even less effective representation in state post-conviction than at the trial stage. The Supreme Court has held that there is no constitutional right to counsel in state post-conviction proceedings, even in capital cases. Although many states and the federal government once funded Post-Conviction Defender Organizations (PCDOs), which recruited lawyers for death row inmates at the post-conviction stage and represented others themselves, today many of those centers have been forced to close because Congress has eliminated their federal funding.

Proper Processes

The ABA consistently has sought to ensure that adequate procedures are in place to determine whether a capital sentence has been entered in violation of federal law. No other organization has monitored the federal *habeas* system more closely, developed greater expertise regarding that system's strengths and weaknesses, or offered more detailed prescriptions for reform.

In 1983, the ABA publicly opposed three bills then pending in Congress that would have dramatically restricted the federal courts' ability to adjudicate state prisoners' *habeas* claims. At the same time, the ABA proposed alternatives that would have streamlined *habeas* litigation without undermining the federal courts' authority and responsibility to exercise independent judgment on the merits of constitutional claims.

Since that time, the ABA has been deeply involved in the national debate over federal *habeas*—particularly in capital cases. The ABA Task Force that studied the situation in depth created a solid scholarly foundation for its work, then received written and oral testimony from knowledgeable individuals and organizations at hearings in several cities. In 1990, the ABA House of Delegates adopted a set of recommendations based upon the task force's work. The recommendations included the principles that a death row prisoner should be entitled to a stay of execution in order to complete one round of post-conviction litigation in state and federal court; that the federal courts should consider claims that were not properly raised in state court if the reason for the prisoner's default was counsel's ignorance or neglect; and that a prisoner should be permitted to file a second or successive federal petition if it raises a new claim

"Grossly unqualified and undercompensated lawyers who have nothing like the support necessary to mount an adequate defense are often appointed to represent capital clients."

that undermines confidence in his or her guilt or the appropriateness of the death sentence.

Regrettably, none of these recommendations has been generally adopted. Instead, the Supreme Court has denied death row prisoners the very opportunities for raising constitutional claims that the ABA has insisted are essential. For example, the federal courts typically have refused to consider claims that were not properly raised in state court, even if the failure to raise them was due to the ignorance or neglect of defense counsel. And prisoners have often not been allowed to litigate more than one petition, even if they have offered strong evidence of egregious constitutional violations that they could not have presented earlier.

"Whatever you think about the death penalty, a system that will take life must first give justice."

The consequence of these legal tangles has been that meritorious constitutional claims often have gone without remedy. Contrary to popular belief, most *habeas* petitions in death penalty cases do not rest on frivolous technicalities. As Professor James S. Liebman has reported, in 40 percent of all capital cases, even in the face of all the procedural barriers, death row inmates still have been able to secure relief due to violations of their basic constitutional rights. The percentage securing relief would be substantially higher if the federal courts had considered all death row inmates' claims on their merits.

Yet, in 1996, Congress enacted legislation that will make it even more difficult for the federal courts to adjudicate federal claims in capital cases. This new law, which the ABA vigorously opposed, establishes deadlines for filing federal *habeas* petitions—deadlines that can run out even when a prisoner has no counsel for a state post-conviction proceeding; limits on federal evidentiary hearings into the facts underlying federal claims; limits on the availability of appellate review; and even more demanding restrictions on second or successive applications from a single petitioner. . . .

Executions Should Be Discontinued

As former ABA President John J. Curtin, Jr., told a congressional committee in 1991, "Whatever you think about the death penalty, a system that will take life must first give justice."

For many years, the ABA has conducted studies, held educational programs, and produced studies and law review articles about the administration of the death penalty. As a result of that work, the Association has identified numerous, critical flaws in current practices. Those flaws have not been redressed; indeed, they have become more severe in recent years, and the new federal *habeas* law and the defunding of the PCDO's have compounded these problems. This situation requires the specific conclusion of the ABA that executions not continue, unless and until greater fairness and due process prevail in death penalty implementation.

Reforms Are Needed to Prevent the Execution of Innocent People

by Craig Aaron

About the author: *Craig Aaron is the features editor of* In These Times, *a biweekly progressive news and opinion journal.*

By the time you are reading this, the United States has probably executed its five hundredth prisoner since 1976. If not, it's just a matter of days before Oklahoma, Texas, South Carolina or Arkansas straps Tuan Nguyen, Joseph Faulder, Joe Truesdale, Robert Robbins or another of the nation's more than 3,500 death row inmates onto the gurney or into the electric chair and kills them.

Number 500 easily could have been any one of the 29 former death row inmates who nervously lined up backstage at the National Conference of Wrongful Convictions and the Death Penalty on Nov. 14, 1998. Each of these men and women were once sentenced to die; some came within hours of being executed—all were innocent. They each spent years, and sometimes decades, on death row for crimes they didn't commit. Only with a stroke of lottery-like luck, divine intervention and a few good lawyers were they freed. One by one, they marched onto the stage, stepped up to the microphone and told the crowd, "If the state had gotten its way, I'd be dead today."

More than 1,000 lawyers, law students, scholars, investigators, journalists and people in "Free Mumia" T-shirts, gathered to hear from the wrongfully convicted at Northwestern University Law School in Chicago for the three-day conference, one of the most important, uplifting and well-publicized anti-death penalty events of the decade. Conference organizers hoped to present the face of "the real death penalty" to counteract the fact that, in theory at least, two-thirds of Americans support capital punishment. The conference dramatically demonstrated that, in practice, the death penalty isn't just reserved for the Ted Bundys and John Wayne Gacys—it also condemns innocent people like Gary

Reprinted, with permission, from "Criminal Injustice System," by Craig Aaron, *In These Times*, December 27, 1998.

Gauger, Freddie Pitts and Walter McMillian.

Indeed, since the Supreme Court overturned *Furman v. Georgia* in 1976 and reinstated the death penalty, 75 death row inmates have been completely exonerated and released. That means that for every 7 prisoners executed, one was set free. The stories of each of these men and women are a powerful testament to the fallibility of the criminal justice system. They also suggest a path of reform. Since the United States isn't ready yet for outright abolition, death penalty opponents should pursue pragmatic, sensible reforms that could make the system fairer and more equal—and save lives.

Harrowing Stories

The stories of the wrongfully convicted are overwhelming. Most involve some combination of incompetent defense lawyers, bloodthirsty or corrupt prosecutors, hanging judges, police beatings, hidden evidence or false testimony. Many are stories of simply being in the wrong place at the wrong time, poor or black: "We need someone for this," a police officer told Clarence Brandley, who was wrongfully convicted for rape and murder in Texas in 1980. "Since you're the nigger, you're elected."

The wrongfully convicted tell of sitting in closet-sized cells for 23 hours a day, writing out legal briefs longhand with a dull pencil and fighting off the roaches and mice for table scraps; they speak of the endless waiting, always thinking about burning alive in the electric chair or being stuck with a lethal needle. "I just wanted to curl up in a ball, scream and holler and bang my head against the wall," says Carl Lawson, who spent six years on Illinois' death row. "I thought, I'd rather be dead than live here in this cell. I felt like the whole world hated me. I had to push so hard to keep from killing myself."

Even freedom comes with a price. After years in prison, most of the wrongfully convicted have struggled on the outside without any skills, job prospects or compensation from the state. Topping it off, they have been held up as examples of how the system works. Try telling that to James Richardson, who was on death row for 21 years. Or Sonia Jacobs: After spending 16 years in prison for the murder of two policemen, it was exposed that prosecution witnesses had lied at her trial. She was released in 1992. Her common-law husband, Jesse Tafero, wasn't so lucky. Convicted on much of the same evidence, he was executed in 1990 before the new information came to light. "These men and women were not released because of the system," says Michael Radelet, co-author of *In Spite of Innocence,* a book about the wrongfully convicted, which documents 23 cases of the innocent being executed this century. "They were released in spite of it."

> ***"Perhaps the most dubious evidence used to send prisoners to death row is the testimony of jailhouse snitches."***

To appreciate the impact of these stories, consider Illinois: Since 1987, nine inmates on the state's death row have been freed. Their cases have created a new awareness of wrongful convictions and official misconduct. Northwestern law professor Larry Marshall, who helped free several of the men and was the driving force behind the Chicago conference, reports a feeling that many trial courts and juries are being more careful than they used to be. In 1997, the Illinois Supreme Court granted some form of relief in half of the capital cases before it—an extremely high percentage compared to other states. And, just a week before the conference, Illinois Supreme Court Justice Moses Harrison wrote a scalding opinion about the state's handling of capital cases. "If these men dodged the executioner, it was only because of luck and the dedication of the attorneys, reporters, family members and volunteers who labored to win their release," he wrote. "The truth is that left to the devices of the court system, they would probably have all ended up dead at the hands of the state for crimes they did not commit. One must wonder how many others have not been so fortunate."

"Among death row inmates, cases of incompetent lawyers failing to interview key witnesses, challenge flawed forensic evidence or mount even a basic defense are a dime a dozen."

The impact of these cases goes beyond the courtroom. Republican Gov. Jim Edgar signed a bill in 1997 that gave prisoners the right to post-conviction DNA testing. And, following the February 1997 call by the American Bar Association for a halt to executions until states can ensure greater fairness and due process, the Illinois legislature is now considering a one-year moratorium.

Emphasizing Fairness

Of course, the only way to ensure that no innocent person is executed is to abolish capital punishment altogether. That remains a noble goal, but it's unachievable in the current political climate. Clearly however, issues of innocence, equality and fairness resonate with the public. Using the example of the wrongfully convicted as a springboard and focusing on the realities of the death penalty, opponents should push for specific, achievable systemic and legislative reforms. "We have to get back to putting fairness ahead of finality," says attorney Steven Bright, director of the Southern Center for Human Rights. "We need to get back to achieving equal justice under the law, or we should just sandblast those words right off the front of the Supreme Court building."

First, safeguards are needed before a case ever gets to court. "If you pushed me against the wall and said I could pick one reform and nothing else," says Jay C. Smith, a former high school principal who was wrongfully convicted in Pennsylvania, "it would be to make sure there's an integrity to the initial investigating process. That's what hangs you." In Smith's trial, one of the police investigators hid exculpatory evidence in his attic.

While this type of criminal activity is impossible to regulate, false or coerced confessions—the source of many wrongful convictions—could be prevented by videotaping interrogations. This idea recently got a lot of attention in Chicago, where, after hours of intense questioning, police mistakenly charged two young boys with the murder of an 11-year-old girl. States should follow the example of Minnesota and Alaska, where the entire interrogation process—not just the confession—is recorded. This reform is good for both the prosecution and the defense. "Videotaping interrogations from the very beginning and showing them to juries, Marshall says, "would save us from wrongful convictions and wrongful acquittals."

Once in court, perhaps the most dubious evidence used to send prisoners to death row is the testimony of jailhouse snitches. Nearly a third of the 75 innocent former death row inmates were convicted as a result of false testimony, usually by cellmates looking for reduced sentences or the real perpetrators claiming them as accomplices. This is a more difficult area of reform, because of the strong resistance of prosecutors to any limit on their power. But, in a closely watched case, the 10th U.S. Circuit Court of Appeals in Denver is considering whether prosecutors can legally offer money or reduced sentences in exchange for testimony. Lawyers for Sonya Singleton—a woman sent to jail on the word of a convicted drug dealer, who testified in exchange for a lesser sentence—argue that offering "anything of value" constitutes bribery, even when it's done by the government. A three judge panel recently agreed, challenging decades of legal practice. The case is likely to reach the Supreme Court, and the Justice Department is already lobbying Congress for legislation to protect prosecutors. "If the case has done nothing else," says attorney John Val Wachtel, "it has pointed out to the courts a real evil that is going on. Even if Sonya loses, the principle may win in the long run."

The Quality of Legal Counsel

The most vital factor in whether someone ends up on death row, however, is not the severity of the crime, class or race—it's quality of counsel. Among death row inmates, cases of incompetent lawyers failing to interview key witnesses, challenge flawed forensic evidence or mount even a basic defense are a dime a dozen. Though capital defense proceedings are the legal equivalent of brain surgery, defense attorneys with nothing more than three years of law school and the bar exam behind them can take a life in their hands. Their mistakes at trial often set up insurmountable obstacles on appeal. At the very least, minimum levels of capital defense training and courtroom experience should be required when a life is on the line.

Then there's the problem of funding: A capital defense case requires multiple lawyers, investigators and support staff to give the defense a fair chance against the unlimited resources of the state. This can be extremely expensive: A large Houston law firm spent more than $3 million defending Ricardo Aldape

Guerra, who spent 15 years in Texas prisons for a crime he didn't commit. It took more than $1 million to free Frederico Macias in the same state. Hundreds of death row inmates don't even have lawyers to handle their appeals. The Chicago conference launched an "Innocence Network" linking law schools working on wrongful convictions to help find cases, recruit lawyers and teach law students to do *pro bono* work.

"Speeding up the rate of executions will only lead to more fatal mistakes."

Building a network to investigate and litigate cases of wrongful conviction is even more crucial in the face of political efforts to limit the appeals of death row inmates and speed up the rate of executions. In 1996, Congress placed stricter limits on post-conviction *habeas corpus* appeals in the federal courts—a refuge for the wrongfully convicted—where judges are appointed for life and face less political pressure. Congress also cut funding from the Capital Resource Centers (CRCs), 20 facilities throughout the country that helped to recruit lawyers, coordinate efforts and file well-researched briefs for capital defense cases. Not only did the CRCs provide inmates with an adequate defense, but they helped smooth out the appeals process. Unfortunately, CRCs were too good at defending death row inmates and discovering constitutional errors, so Republicans shut them down. Re-establishing the CRCs is a top legislative priority. While it's a long shot in this Congress, the wrongfully convicted could make excellent lobbyists.

The median length of time it took for the 75 wrongfully convicted death row inmates to be vindicated was 7 years: Speeding up the rate of executions will only lead to more fatal mistakes. "So what if it takes ten years?" asks Randall Adams, the former Texas death row inmate, who was freed after 12 years, thanks in part to the film *A Thin Blue Line.* "At least it's an improvement from when they used to take you out in the street and hang you."

Exonerating Evidence

There is some good news: In recent years, DNA testing has exonerated more than 50 prisoners, including 11 death row inmates. Hundreds more cases are pending. Yet currently only New York and Illinois have laws that provide inmates access to potentially exculpatory biological evidence without limits on cost or time. In fact, according to Amnesty International, more than 30 states mandate time limits on the admissibility of any new exonerating evidence post-conviction; in 12 states, defendants have less than 30 days to introduce new evidence. DNA is the most promising recent development in identifying and freeing the wrongfully convicted, and it's only fair that every state give inmates unfettered access. "It's so important in this debate to look back at the people who we said were guilty as all hell, that through DNA were found to be absolutely innocent," Marshall says. "This is a huge breakthrough in forensics and hundreds, and thousands will be vindicated. If that is the case, how can we be killing anyone who claims an issue of innocence?"

DNA is not a panacea. It isn't even left at most crime scenes. The wrongfully convicted like Rolando Cruz of Illinois and Kirk Bloodsworth of Maryland were able to use DNA evidence to help prove their innocence only because their cases involved rape. However, the high number of recent exonerations thanks to DNA does expose the unreliable nature of some evidence like eyewitness identification.

Some death penalty opponents are critical of a focus on systemic and procedural changes. "We need to be talking less about the struggle within the system and more about the political struggle," says Marlene Martin of the Campaign to End the Death Penalty. "We must challenge the politicians. They know full well that the death penalty is applied in a racist way and that innocent people have been put on death row—they read the papers. We must put pressure on the politicians and understand their instinct to use the death penalty for political gain."

It's true that reforms, systemic and otherwise, will never be implemented without public pressure. From the outside, one of the most powerful arguments against the death penalty is its racial inequality. It's common knowledge that blacks are executed for killing whites, but whites are not executed for murdering blacks. Still, some statistics bear repeating: One study of Philadelphia found the odds of receiving the death penalty are four times higher if the defendant is black. At one point, all 39 people on Kentucky's death row were there for killing a white person, even though a thousand blacks had been killed in the state during the same period. Meanwhile, in the 38 states with capital punishment, 98 percent of prosecutors responsible for the decision to seek death are white, according to a 1996 study by the Death Penalty Information Center.

"The 75 innocent people released from death row serve as a powerful indictment of the criminal justice system."

In March 1998, the outrageous racial disparity spurred passage of the Racial Justice Act in Kentucky, giving defendants the right to introduce statistical and other evidence of racial bias in their defense. Attempts to pass similar legislation in Congress have failed. With Congress paying closer attention to the black vote following the November 1998 election, the time is ripe to push for federal legislation again.

A Larger Crisis

The innocent on death row highlight a much larger crisis. Radelet says the wrongfully convicted also include those who killed accidentally or in self-defense, had improper counsel, have little mental ability, are children or should have been charged with a lesser crime. "What about the innocent doing life, doing two years," Adams adds. "If mistakes can happen with the ultimate penalty, how many other mistakes are happening?"

Some studies suggest that the rate of wrongful conviction for lesser crimes such as sexual abuse is much higher than for murder. "Capital punishment is the capstone in the war against the 'other,'" says Robert Meeropol, a leading activist whose parents, Ethel and Julius Rosenberg, were executed in 1953. "It shows that it is a war, a place where life imprisonment without parole seems humane. If we don't place it in the larger context of the prison industrial complex, we may win a narrow victory, but we lose the larger battle."

Nonetheless, the 75 innocent people released from death row serve as a powerful indictment of the criminal justice system and the continued use of capital punishment. "We are alive today despite the criminal justice system's intense efforts to kill us for crimes we did not commit," reads a statement signed by the former death row inmates at the conference. "It is our fervent hope that society is capable of learning from its mistakes."

Claims About the Unfairness of Capital Punishment Are Unfounded

by Michael Levin

About the author: *Michael Levin is a contributing editor of the* Rothbard-Rockwell Report, *a newsletter published monthly by the Center for Libertarian Studies in Burlingame, California.*

The capital punishment debate is heating up. Because the Bronx District Attorney has vowed never to seek death no matter how heinous the offense, the Governor of New York recently barred him from trying a carjacker who killed a policeman. . . . Not that the average person cares what the American Philosophical Association is up to, but its actions are a good guide to liberal-elite thinking, and I am told it is ready to condemn "legal murder." (One of America's leading abolitionists is a philosophy professor, Hugo Bedau.) It's a good time for friends of liberty to clarify their view of the question.

The State Is Entitled to Kill

As a rule, libertarians mistrust capital punishment because they don't want to cede government the power of life and death. However, once the state is granted the right to administer lesser punishments, it cannot be denied the right to kill. Consider that John Locke, nobody's idea of bloodthirsty, *defined* "political power" as "a right of making laws with penalties of death and, consequently, all less penalties." Why did Locke take infliction of death to be fundamental? Well, the state must be able to enforce whatever it commands, or it is a state in name only. The question then becomes how far it may go to overcome resistance.

If the state has no right to kill, and can press lawbreakers to obey it up to the point of lethality but no further, a lawbreaker can defy the state by resisting so vehemently that only lethal force will bring him to heel. Since the state can't kill him, it must let him have his way. Suppose I won't pay a speeding ticket.

Reprinted, with permission, from "Punishment—Capital!" by Michael Levin, *Rothbard-Rockwell Report*, June 1996.

Agents of the state (hereinafter "the cops") come to my house to collect. I still won't pay. When the cops move to arrest me I pull a gun. At this point they can either shoot me or back off. With no right to shoot me the cops must go home, I have speeded with impunity, and the state has been rendered impotent.

"Once the state is granted the right to administer lesser punishments, it cannot be denied the right to kill."

Once the state is entitled to compel me, it is entitled to do so with lethal force, and once it is granted that right, denying it use of punitive lethal force is straining at a gnat. If you're going to deny the government the right to take life, you might as well repudiate government itself. Libertarians may see no problem here: just cut the Gordian knot and declare government illegitimate. Unfortunately, the basic problem of capital punishment remains. After all, libertarians are committed to rights and the need to protect them; their distinctive idea is that private enforcement, perhaps through contracting agencies, is more efficient than public.

But then the old question comes right back: How far can you or your agency go in constraining the behavior of a perceived rights-violator? Do you have the right to kill him if he won't remove his hand from your pocket? Do you have a right to threaten death for a grievous enough violation of your rights, and follow through? Can you transfer this right to your enforcement agency? Once again, it appears, all your other rights would be nullities without this "executive" right. So libertarians must deal with the same Clausewitzian axiom that leads to state-sponsored executions: the serious use of legitimate force must escalate to the max.

What About Incarceration?

The issue is whether anybody, public or private, has a right to take life. Of the many arguments against this prerogative, the most common is that "death is different." An innocent man executed can't be resurrected—once a mistake is made, that's it. (Abolitionists who admit capital punishment deters usually take this argument to outweigh it.) *But exactly the same is true of incarceration,* the abolitionist's favored alternative.

A 20-year-old man is given a life sentence for a crime he didn't commit. Fifty years later the error is discovered and he is released. Now suppose that all during his life he values five years of freedom over one year of life; that is, he would trade death after five years of confinement for death after four years of liberty. By his lights, the fifty years behind bars have robbed him of ten years of life. Ah, you say, but the error is corrigible, for he still has life left after his release. Yes, *but it may not be enough.* He must live ten more years just to regain the years lost in prison; if he dies at 75, he has lost five years absolutely. As far as he is concerned, he would have lived longer had he been wrongly executed at 65!

The numbers in this example are arbitrary, but the basic point applies to just about everyone. Most of us would forego a little life (a week, say) to avoid a long prison term. That being so, "incarceration is different," and every innocent man imprisoned loses some irreplaceable life.

Other Abolitionist Arguments

A second ploy popular with abolitionists is the cost and delay of execution. Right now it takes on average 12 years to execute a condemned man. The seemingly endless appeals process costs taxpayers more than $1 million per case. But executions are costly and time-consuming precisely because of abolitionist obstructionism—and it is absurd to oppose a policy on grounds of cost and then explain that it is costly because you oppose it. The abolitionist has been compared to a man who advises you that your watch is defective, and, when asked why, points out the glue he has poured into the works.

Next comes race; capital punishment is said to discriminate against blacks. Actually, liberals think everything discriminates, and that society should come to a screeching halt until this ubiquitous evil has been ended. Since bias-spotters see discrimination everywhere, their conclusions about the justice system—which they scrutinize closely and selectively—are a bit confusing. Especially harsh penalties for crimes involving the crack form of cocaine were once demanded to stop crack from "decimating the inner cities." When the overwhelming majority of crack criminals turned out to be black, these same statutes were condemned as racist.

Now, the abolitionist complaint about capital punishment is not that blacks are executed at a higher rate than whites, since blacks commit murders at a higher rate than whites, and in fact the ratio of black to white murderers exceeds the black/white ratio on death row. The complaint, rather, is that murderers of whites are more likely to receive the death penalty than murderers of blacks.

The statistical support for this is unimpressive. One study using data from Georgia for 1979–1982 claimed that killers of whites were executed 6% more frequently when type of homicide is held constant; other experts told the Senate Judiciary Committee (which held hearings on the question in 1992) that the discrepancy vanishes when other factors, like previous sentencing history, are controlled for.

To my mind a discrepancy as small as 6%, even if genuine, does not show that "society values white lives more than black" (a favorite liberal slogan), and in any case the discrepancy is best explained by race differences in temperament. No one denies that blacks are more impulsive than whites (although whites somehow get blamed for this), and blacks also appear to be less empathetic. The greater impulsivity means that blacks commit proportionally more non-capital homicides than whites—of family members during quarrels, of acquaintances in bar fights, and the like.

The race of the victim of such impulse-killings is almost always that of the perpetrator, so blacks are disproportionately often the *victims* of non-capital homicides. On the other hand, murders committed in the course of a felony are usually capitalized, and not only do black felons commit most of the armed robberies and murders in the US, they are much more apt to pick a white victim than a white felon is to pick a black victim. (3% of white crimes are committed against blacks, while half of all black crimes are committed against whites.)

It is not just that blacks are much more likely to murder whites than vice-versa, although this is indeed so: In Georgia between 1979 and 1982, when bias was supposed to be operating against blacks, 233 whites were murdered by blacks while 60 blacks were murdered by whites. (Since blacks make up 26% of the population of Georgia, this means that blacks murdered whites more than seven times as frequently as whites murdered blacks.) The important point is that lower levels of empathy mean that blacks are more likely to kill felony victims—out of a desire to remove witnesses, frustration at getting too little money, or bravado. Consequently, a white is more likely than a black to *be* a victim of a felony murder that carries the death sentence.

"Blacks are much more likely to murder whites than vice-versa."

Ultimately, abolitionism strangles on its own internal contradictions. If killing is not so terrible that murderers deserve to die, then killing is not too terrible for the state—or enforcement agencies—to undertake. If killing is as terrible as abolitionists say, if it really is an act of boundless, unredeemable horror, the murderer has committed an act of boundless, unredeemable horror—in which case, one would think, he has lost his right to life. Abolitionists seem to take the position that felony murders are not the worst thing imaginable: executions are.

Deterrence

I have avoided the topic of deterrence to focus on moral issues, and because, to my knowledge, the statistics are ambiguous. That the prospect of dying does deter seems pretty obvious to me, and if death penalty statistics don't reflect this, the delay and uncertainty in its application is probably why. What interests me most about deterrence is what is revealed by the attitude of liberals towards it. I'm not thinking mainly of those who admit imprisonment deters but deny that a swift and sure death penalty does (I'm not convinced anyone actually believes this), or those who don't care whether death deters or not. I'm thinking of the ones who confidently announce that "punishment doesn't deter."

This is one of those rare cases in which a popular opinion comes apart as soon as one thinks about what it means. A punishment, after all, is simply a stimulus that makes less likely any behavior with which it is associated. In economic language, a punishment lowers the value of anything it is associated with. It is the cost of behavior. So, *by definition,* a punishment deters. In other words, what liberals mean when they announce that punishment doesn't deter is that *there is no such thing as punishment.*

The only reason I can imagine for someone saying something so absurd is wish-fulfillment: liberals don't think it is true, but they would like it to be. The fact is, liberal abolitionists just don't like to see wrong-doers suffer. Liberals opposed to capital punishment usually offer life-without-parole in its stead. But then they bemoan the pointlessness of incarcerating harmless 80-year-olds with heart conditions, the expense of such incarceration, how three-strikes-you're-in laws are turning prisons into geriatric wards. . . .

In his heart no liberal likes life without parole. He is not even for long sentences. Let a murderer jailed for 25 years (and preferably belonging to a racial minority) learn to read, and, if he has not killed anyone else in the meanwhile, liberals will demand his release. He could be a constructive member of society, they will clamor; keeping him locked up does no good—with liberals ever oblivious to the effect of releasing murderers on the future credibility of long sentences. It's true. Liberals think innocent people, capitalists, and "society" are the true criminals, and murderers their innocent victims. They really do think executing a murderer is worse than murdering a child.

Except, except. . . . There is one argument which, while it will not get a liberal to endorse capital punishment, is guaranteed to disarm his opposition, as well as bring perspiration to his brow. And this argument has the added virtue of being only syllables long. I offer it to you: Tim McVeigh. [McVeigh was sentenced to death for the 1995 bombing of a federal office building in Oklahoma City.]

I've kept a careful eye out, and none of the usual abolitionist institutions—the *New York Times,* the *Washington Post,* the American Civil Liberties Union, Susan Sarandon—has said word one about sparing him. He's white, he's sort of right wing, and he is not a victim of mistaken identity. As an experiment, ask any liberal of your acquaintance whether McVeigh should be executed. You'll see squirming, you'll see dancing around the issue, but you won't hear that McVeigh is "sick" and you won't get a flat-out declaration that he should be spared. That cri de coeur is reserved for cop-killers and child molesters.

> ***"A white is more likely than a black to* be *a victim of a felony murder that carries the death sentence."***

Capital Punishment Is Not Applied Unfairly to Blacks

by Jeff Jacoby

About the author: *Jeff Jacoby is a nationally syndicated columnist.*

Death penalty opponents frequently argue that capital punishment is racist, meted out disproportionately to blacks, especially blacks who kill whites. If there is any city where that argument ought to hold sway, it is Washington, D.C., an overwhelmingly black community that is acutely sensitive to questions of racial justice.

Indeed, until recently, Washingtonians were solidly against the death penalty. A 1992 ballot measure to establish capital punishment in the district was crushed by a ratio of 2 to 1. Among the leading opponents was Marion Barry, the once and future mayor, who forested D.C. neighborhoods with signs proclaiming, "Thou Shalt Not Kill."

But five years later, Washington residents—particularly its black residents, who comprise more than two-thirds of the city's population—are having second thoughts.

According to a new *Washington Post* poll, 52 percent of D.C. voters now agree that murderers should be executed, and 59 percent support the death penalty for those convicted of killing police officers. Among African-Americans, the change of heart is especially pronounced: 55 percent of black D.C. residents polled favor the death penalty generally, and 64 percent—nearly 2 out of 3—favor it for those who kill police. Legislation to authorize capital punishment has been proposed anew, and one of its key backers is—Marion Barry.

This turnaround is remarkable. Washington's black citizens have more reason than most to be wary of the criminal justice system. At any given time in the District of Columbia, more than 40 percent of black men aged 18 to 34 are in trouble with the law. An estimated 70 percent of black men in Washington will be arrested before their 35th birthday. Barry himself went to prison on a drug conviction after being entrapped in an FBI sting operation.

Reprinted, with permission, from "Without Death Penalty, More Black Victims Die," by Jeff Jacoby, *Conservative Chronicle*, May 28, 1997.

Yet if the *Post* survey is accurate, none of this any longer dissuades black Washingtonians from supporting capital punishment. Like residents of other violence-ridden cities, they are sick of living in a war zone. Behind the white marble temples, the District of Columbia has one of the highest murder rates in the nation, and its residents have finally come to see what most Americans already intuit: When murderers live, innocent people die.

Fueling Mistrust Between the Races

Of all the arguments raised against the death penalty, the racial justice claim is the ugliest. Not because it is false, but because it is designed to fuel mistrust and cynicism between races—then use that ill will as a reason not to execute murderers. Hear Helen Prejean, the author of *Dead Man Walking* and an anti-death penalty crusader: "Middle and upper-middle-class white people," she told an interviewer, "are so much for the death penalty" because they want to repress African-Americans. Whites may talk about law and justice, she said, but what they're really thinking is: "Keep those dangerous people"—black people—"in their place." That isn't an argument about capital punishment. It's an incitement to race hatred.

The notion that inmates on death row are usually poor African-Americans is sheer propaganda. There are more whites than blacks on death row. Each year more whites than blacks are executed. If there is a shocking racial disparity anywhere, it is not in the punishing but in the committing of murder: Blacks comprise only 12 percent of the population, yet 50 percent of all homicides are committed by blacks.

Death penalty data are not in dispute: In 1995, 33 of the 56 murderers executed in the United States were white. In 1994, 20 out of 31. In the two decades since capital punishment was re-authorized by the Supreme Court, 313 inmates have been executed. Fifty-five percent have been white; 38 percent have been black. White murderers are more likely to be executed than black murderers, and have been since at least 1929. If there is racism on death row, it is certainly well disguised.

> ***"The notion that inmates on death row are usually poor African-Americans is sheer propaganda. There are more whites than blacks on death row."***

It is true, as death penalty opponents point out, that a sentence of death is more often handed down in cases where the victim was white. The implication is that in a racially fair justice system, the murderers of blacks would get the death penalty just as frequently as the murderers of whites. But the vast majority of black homicide is intra-racial—93 percent of African-American murder victims are killed by African-Americans. If "racial justice" means executing more of those who murder blacks, then it means sending more black men to the chair. Is that what the critics seek?

Of course it isn't. What the critics seek isn't a "racially just" death penalty, it's no death penalty at all—not for whites, not for blacks, not for cop-killers, not for terrorists, not for mass murderers, not for anybody. And the truth is, they have gotten their way. For all intents and purposes, there is no death penalty in the United States—not when more than 20,000 victims are slaughtered each year, and 99.9 percent of their killers are permitted to live.

"If there is racism on death row, it is certainly well disguised."

The price of letting murderers live is that more innocent people die. And they die most violently and tragically in America's black precincts. Homicide is by far the leading cause of death among young African-Americans. Four hundred human beings were murdered in Washington, D.C., in 1996. Four hundred human beings, on average, are murdered in Washington every year. So long as killers know that they can take a life and not forfeit their own, the killing will go on.

Unfair Application of Capital Punishment Does Not Justify Abolishing It

by Louis P. Pojman

About the author: *Louis P. Pojman is the author or editor of over twenty books and seventy-five articles. He teaches at the United States Military Academy in West Point, New York.*

Let us examine some of the major objections to capital punishment, as well as the retentionist's responses to those objections.

1. *Objection:* Capital punishment is a morally unacceptable thirst for revenge. As former British Prime Minister Edward Heath put it,

> The real point which is emphasized to me by many constituents is that even if the death penalty is not a deterrent, murderers deserve to die. This is the question of revenge. Again, this will be a matter of moral judgment for each of us. I do not believe in revenge. If I were to become the victim of terrorists, I would not wish them to be hanged or killed in any other way for revenge. All that would do is deepen the bitterness which already tragically exists in the conflicts we experience in society, particularly in Northern Ireland.

Response: Retributivism is not the same thing as revenge, although the two attitudes are often intermixed in practice. Revenge is a personal response to a perpetrator for an injury. Retribution is an impartial and impersonal response to an offender for an offense done against someone. You cannot desire revenge for the harm of someone to whom you are indifferent. Revenge always involves personal concern for the victim. Retribution is not personal but based on objective factors: the criminal has deliberately harmed an innocent party and so *deserves* to be punished, whether I wish it or not. I would agree that I or my son or daughter *deserves* to be punished for our crimes, but I don't wish any vengeance on myself or my son or daughter.

Furthermore, while revenge often leads us to exact more suffering from the

Excerpted from "For the Death Penalty," by Louis P. Pojman, in *The Death Penalty: For and Against*, by Louis P. Pojman and Jeffrey Reiman.

offender than the offense warrants, retribution stipulates that the offender be punished in proportion to the gravity of the offense. In this sense, the *lex talionis* which we find in the Old Testament is actually a progressive rule, where retribution replaces revenge as the mode of punishment. It says that there are limits to what one may do to the offender. Revenge demands a life for an eye or a tooth, but Moses provides a rule that exacts a penalty equal to the harm done by the offender.

> ***"Society has a right to protect itself from capital offenses even if this means taking a finite chance of executing an innocent person."***

2. *Objection:* Perhaps the murderer does deserve to die, but by what authority does the state execute him or her? Both the Old and New Testament says, "'Vengeance is mine, I will repay,' says the Lord" (Prov. 25:21 and Romans 12:19). You need special authority to justify taking the life of a human being.

Response: The objector fails to note that the New Testament passage continues with a support of the right of the state to execute criminals in the name of God: "Let every person be subjected to the governing authorities. For there is no authority except from God, and those that exist have been instituted by God. Therefore he who resists what God has appointed, and those who resist will incur judgment. . . . If you do wrong, be afraid, for [the authority] does not bear the sword in vain; he is the servant of God to execute his wrath on the wrongdoer" (Romans 13:1–4). So, according to the Bible, the authority to punish, which presumably includes the death penalty, comes from God.

But we need not appeal to a religious justification for capital punishment. We can cite the state's role in dispensing justice. Just as the state has the authority (and duty) to act justly in allocating scarce resources, in meeting minimal needs of its (deserving) citizens, in defending its citizens from violence and crime, and in not waging unjust wars; so too does it have the authority, flowing from its mission to promote justice and the good of its people, to punish the criminal. If the criminal, as one who has forfeited a right to life, deserves to be executed, especially if it will likely deter would-be murderers, the state has a duty to execute those convicted of first-degree murder.

What About Miscarriages of Justice?

3. *Objection:* Miscarriages of justice occur. Capital punishment is to be rejected because of human fallibility in convicting innocent parties and sentencing them to death. In a survey done in 1985 Hugo Adam Bedau and Michael Radelet found that of the 7,000 persons executed in the United States between 1900 and 1985, 25 were innocent of capital crimes. While some compensation is available to those unjustly imprisoned, the death sentence is irrevocable. We can't compensate the dead. As John Maxton, a member of the British Parliament puts it, "If we allow one innocent person to be executed, morally we are

committing the same, or, in some ways, a worse crime than the person who committed the murder.

Response: Mr. Maxton is incorrect in saying that mistaken judicial execution is morally the same or worse than murder, for a deliberate intention to kill the innocent occurs in a murder, whereas no such intention occurs in wrongful capital punishment.

Sometimes this objection is framed this way: It is better to let ten criminals go free than to execute one innocent person. If this dictum is a call for safeguards, then it is well taken; but somewhere there seems to be a limit on the tolerance of society towards capital offenses. Would these abolitionists argue that it is better that 50 or 100 or 1,000 murderers go free than that one guilty person be executed? Society has a right to protect itself from capital offenses even if this means taking a finite chance of executing an innocent person. If the basic activity or process is justified, then it is regrettable, but morally acceptable, that some mistakes are made. Fire trucks occasionally kill innocent pedestrians while racing to fires, but we accept these losses as justified by the greater good of the activity of using fire trucks. We judge the use of automobiles to be acceptable even though such use causes an average of 50,000 traffic fatalities each year. We accept the morality of a defensive war even though it will result in our troops accidentally or mistakenly killing innocent people.

The fact that we can err in applying the death penalty should give us pause and cause us to build an appeals process into the judicial system. Such a process is already in the American and British legal systems. That occasional error may be made, regrettable though this is, is not a sufficient reason for us to refuse to use the death penalty, if on balance it serves a just and useful function.

Are Prison Sentences a Good Alternative?

Furthermore, abolitionists are simply misguided in thinking that prison sentences are a satisfactory alternative here. It's not clear that we can always or typically compensate innocent parties who waste away in prison. Jacques Barzun has argued that a prison sentence can be worse than death and carries all the problems that the death penalty does regarding the impossibility of compensation:

> In the preface of his useful volume of cases, *Hanged in Error,* Mr. Leslie Hale refers to the tardy recognition of a minor miscarriage of justice—one year in jail: "The prisoner emerged to find that his wife had died and that his children and his aged parents had been removed to the workhouse. By the time a small payment had been assessed as 'compensation' the victim was incurably insane." So far we are as indignant with the law as Mr. Hale. But what comes next? He cites the famous Evans case, in which it is very probable that the wrong man was hanged, and he exclaims: "While such mistakes are possible, should society impose an irrevocable sentence?" Does Mr. Hale really ask us to believe that the sentence passed on the first man, whose wife died and who went insane, was in any sense *revocable*? Would not any man rather be Evans

> dead than that other wretch "emerging" with his small compensation and his reason for living gone?

The abolitionist is incorrect in arguing that death is different than long-term prison sentences because it is irrevocable. Imprisonment also takes good things away from us that may never be returned. We cannot restore to the inmate the freedom or opportunities he or she lost. Suppose an innocent 25-year-old man is given a life sentence for murder. Thirty years later the mistake is discovered and he is set free. Suppose he values three years of freedom to every one year of prison life. That is, he would rather live ten years as a free man than thirty as a prisoner. Given this man's values, the criminal justice system has taken the equivalent of ten years of life from him. If he lives until he is 65, he has, as far as his estimation is concerned, lost ten years, so that he may be said to have lived only 55 years.

The numbers in this example are arbitrary, but the basic point is sound. Most of us would prefer a shorter life of higher quality to a longer one of low quality. Death prevents all subsequent quality, but imprisonment also irrevocably harms one in diminishing the quality of life of the prisoner.

Unequal Justice Is Still Justice

4. *Objection:* The death penalty is unjust because it discriminates against the poor and minorities, particularly, African Americans, over rich people and whites. Former Supreme Court Justice William Douglas wrote that "a law which reaches that [discriminatory] result in practice has no more sanctity than a law which in terms provides the same." Stephen Nathanson, author of *An Eye for an Eye?,* argues that "in many cases, whether one is treated justly or not depends not only on what one deserves but on how other people are treated." He offers the example of unequal justice in a plagiarism case. "I tell the students in my class that anyone who plagiarizes will fail the course. Three students plagiarize papers, but I give only one a failing grade. The other two, in describing their motivation, win my sympathy, and I give them passing grades." Arguing that this is patently unjust, he likens this case to the imposition of the death penalty and concludes that it too is unjust.

> ***"It is not true that a law that is applied in a discriminatory manner is unjust."***

Response: First of all, it is not true that a law that is applied in a discriminatory manner is unjust. Unequal justice is no less justice, however uneven its application. The discriminatory application, not the law itself, is unjust. A just law is still just even if it is not applied consistently. For example, a friend of mine once got two speeding tickets during a 100-mile trip (having borrowed my car). He complained to the police officer who gave him his second ticket that many drivers were driving faster than he was at the time. They had escaped detection, he argued, so it wasn't fair for him to get two tickets on one trip. The officer acknowledged the imperfections of the system but, justifiably, had no qualms about giving him the second ticket. Unequal justice is still justice, however regrettable. So Justice Douglas is wrong in asserting that discriminatory results invalidate the law itself. The discriminatory practice should be reformed, and in many cases it can be. But imperfect practices in themselves do not entail that the laws engendering these practices are themselves unjust.

"Imperfect justice is the best that we humans can attain."

With regard to Nathanson's analogy with the plagiarism case, two things should be said against it. First, if the teacher is convinced that the motivational factors are mitigating factors, then he or she may be justified in passing two of the plagiarizing students. Suppose that the one student did no work whatsoever, showed no interest (Nathanson's motivation factor) in learning, and exhibited no remorse in cheating, whereas the other two spent long hours seriously studying the material and, upon apprehension, showed genuine remorse for their misdeeds. To be sure, they yielded to temptation at certain—though limited—sections of their long papers, but the vast majority of their papers represented their own diligent work. Suppose, as well, that all three had C averages at this point. The teacher gives the unremorseful, gross plagiarizer an F but relents and gives the other two D's. Her actions parallel the judge's use of mitigating circumstances and cannot be construed as arbitrary, let alone unjust.

The second problem with Nathanson's analogy is that it would have disastrous consequences for all law and benevolent practices alike. If we concluded that we should abolish a rule or practice, unless we treated everyone exactly by the same rules all the time, we would have to abolish, for example, traffic laws and laws against imprisonment for rape, theft, and even murder. Carried to its logical limits, we would also have to refrain from saving drowning victims if a number of people were drowning but we could only save a few of them. Imperfect justice is the best that we humans can attain. We should reform our practices as much as possible to eradicate unjust discrimination wherever we can, but if we are not allowed to have a law without perfect application, we will be forced to have no laws at all.

Nathanson acknowledges this latter response but argues that the case of death is different. "Because of its finality and extreme severity of the death penalty, we need to be more scrupulous in applying it as punishment than is necessary with any other punishment." The retentionist agrees that the death penalty is a severe punishment and that we need to be scrupulous in applying it. The difference between the abolitionist and the retentionist seems to lie in whether we are wise and committed enough as a nation to reform our institutions so that they approximate fairness. Apparently, Nathanson is pessimistic here, whereas I have faith in our ability to learn from our mistakes and reform our systems. If we can't reform our legal system, what hope is there for us?

More specifically, the charge that a higher percentage of blacks than whites are executed was once true but is no longer so. Many states have made significant changes in sentencing procedures, with the result that currently whites convicted of first-degree murder are sentenced to death at a higher rate than blacks.

One must be careful in reading too much into these statistics. While great disparities in statistics should cause us to examine our judicial procedures, they do not in themselves prove injustice. For example, more males than females are convicted of violent crimes (almost 90% of those convicted of violent crimes are males—a virtually universal statistic), but this is not strong evidence that the law is unfair, for there are psychological explanations for the disparity in convictions. Males are on average and by nature more aggressive (usually tied to testosterone) than females. Likewise, there may be good explanations why people of one ethnic group commit more crimes than those of other groups, explanations which do not impugn the processes of the judicial system.

The Death Penalty Should Be Carried Out More Promptly

by David Frum

About the author: *David Frum is a contributing editor of the* Weekly Standard, *a conservative journal of opinion.*

The co-perpetrator of the worst terrorist attack in American history; a woman convicted of pick-axing two sleeping people to death; a cold-blooded mail-bomber on trial for two murders and two maimings: These are some of the people who have convinced sympathetic listeners that they ought to escape the maximum legal punishment for their crimes. The death penalty is unequivocally constitutional. It is supported by a crushing majority of the American people. Moralists from the authors of the Bible to John Stuart Mill have regarded it as just. And yet somehow Americans encounter the most enormous difficulty persuading their justice system to put it into effect.

Every year the newspapers run stories about the rapid rise in criminal executions in the United States. Spread over half a dozen columns, illustrated with charts that show death sentences rocketing upward like the Dow Jones industrial average, they present an image of a country grimly bent on snuffing out as many lives as possible. The *Washington Post* offered a fine example of the genre on December 15, 1997 in a story observing that the number of executions nationally hit a four-decade high in 1997 and that Virginia executed more people than it had in any year since 1909. "I think the death machinery has kicked into high gear," the *Post* quoted the director of the American Civil Liberties Union's Capital Punishment Project as saying.

You'd think that the whole United States was crackling with the sound of the electric chair. But as so often, the newspaper stories are misleading. No, they're not literally dishonest. It is indeed true that in 1997 the United States executed twice as many criminals as in 1994, that it executed twice as many in 1994 as it

Reprinted, with permission, from "The Truth About the Chair," by David Frum, *The Weekly Standard*, January 19, 1998. Copyright, News America Inc.

had in 1989, and three times as many in 1989 as in 1983. That's one way to tell the story. But here's another: At no point in the [decades] since the Supreme Court reauthorized the death penalty [in 1976] has the number of murderers executed in this country exceeded the number of Americans killed by lightning.

In 1997, 74 killers were put to death, bringing the total number of executions in the United States since capital punishment resumed to 432. Over the same two decades, nearly 500,000 Americans were murdered. Assuming that most killers kill only once, the average murderer has faced a less than one in 1,000 chance of suffering the maximum theoretical legal punishment for the taking of innocent life. Let's put it this way: Committing a murder in the United States today is almost nine times safer than being drafted during the Vietnam War; the 11 million men inducted between 1965 and 1973 faced a one in 130 chance of dying in Indochina. You often hear it said that the death penalty doesn't deter. If not, it may be because, from the point of view of a killer, execution is a contingency as remote and hypothetical as going to hell. Rather more remote and hypothetical, actually.

Americans are now congratulating themselves on the spectacular fall in crime over the past three or four years. It is genuinely impressive. But it's worth remembering that today's crime rates have fallen back only to the levels that prevailed in the late 1970s (or, in the case of star pupil New York City, the late 1960s)—levels that were at the time viewed as shocking and outrageous. By world standards, by the standards of America's own history, this country remains a terrifyingly dangerous place. Perhaps one reason that the country used not to be so dangerous was the greater willingness of courts in those days to sentence the most heinous offenders to the ultimate punishment. In the 1930s, when Harlemites could sleep on their fire escapes, the country executed between 150 and 200 criminals *per year.*

> ***"Americans encounter the most enormous difficulty persuading their justice system to put [the death penalty] into effect."***

It is often said that the death penalty is rare because juries are reluctant to impose it: Seeing a human being in the dock, they cannot bring themselves to condemn him to death. That's untrue. From the beginning of 1977 through the end of 1996, American state and federal juries condemned more than 5,500 murderers to death. At trial, jurors are required to look the defendant in the eye, while the crime can be conjured up only by immaterial words and sorry little scraps of admissible evidence. But even so, when they encounter an atrocious crime, jurors are generally willing to enforce the law. No, it's not juries that have made the death penalty an arbitrary, freak occurrence; it's the determination of a small band of activist lawyers to thwart the commands of the law, and the even more troubling willingness of the courts to let the law be thwarted.

Nor—despite the rise in the aggregate number of executions—has this unwillingness to apply the law abated in recent years. The length of time it takes to carry out a death sentence has steadily risen since 1976: The criminals executed in 1985 had spent an average of six years on death row; the criminals executed in 1990 had spent an average of eight and a quarter years; the criminals executed in 1996 had spent an average of ten and a half years.

Death-penalty opponents like to posit a choice: in the words of an August 1997 Gallup poll, "the death penalty or life in prison with absolutely no possibility of parole." In fact, no such choice exists. The people who administer the American justice system are not only reluctant to carry out death sentences, they cannot bring themselves to carry out life sentences either.

> ***"The criminals executed in 1996 had spent an average of ten and a half years [on death row]."***

Despite the half-million slayings since 1976, there are—as criminologist John DiIulio points out—only about 100,000 killers in prison today. In other words, some 70 percent of the men and women who have killed a spouse, child, friend, or neighbor over the past two decades have either been released from prison or never went in the first place. The average killer, by DiIulio's estimate, spends just eight and a half years in jail.

Nobody can deny that there is something capricious about the way the death penalty is applied in America today. There are states, like New York, with death penalties on the books that have been cunningly written to ensure that nobody will ever actually receive a capital sentence. There are states, like Pennsylvania, where criminals are frequently sentenced to death, but where the sentences somehow are never put into effect. Even the apparent rise in executions in 1997 turns out to be a fluke. Remove one state, Texas, from the total, and the number of executions in the other 49 actually dropped below that in 1996. All together, 94 percent of the killers sentenced to death since 1976 have thus far evaded the punishment meted out to them by judge and jury.

The right way to deal with that capriciousness, however, is to ensure that the death sentence, when lawfully imposed, is promptly carried out, and not—as death-penalty critics argue—to abandon it in the hope that if we do, the justice system will suddenly start enforcing genuine life sentences. The zeal of death-penalty opponents for life imprisonment without parole will last exactly as long as the death penalty remains legal. It remains true that any attempt to punish crime severely—whether by execution or by life imprisonment—generates intense opposition. The death penalty excites that opposition more fiercely than anything else right now, but if the death penalty were done away with, the locus of opposition to punishment would shift to the alleged inhumanity of "throwing away the key." Substantial numbers of people with the power to disrupt the operation of the criminal-justice system still believe that crime is a symptom of social injustice and that criminals should be cured rather than punished. The death penalty may be the top item on their agenda, but it is not the last.

Chapter 3

Is Capital Punishment an Effective Deterrent to Crime?

The Death Penalty and Deterrence: An Overview

by Richard L. Worsnop

About the author: *Richard L. Worsnop is a staff writer for* CQ Researcher, *a weekly report on current issues.*

Capital punishment backers traditionally cite two reasons why society is justified in executing certain criminals: retribution and deterrence. They claim that executions satisfy the public's demand that murderers suffer punishment proportionate to their offense. The deterrence rationale rests on somewhat shakier ground, however, because of the difficulty of proving that the death penalty deters capital crimes.

Nonetheless, deterrence is invariably part of the debate. A 1985 study by Stephen K. Layson, an economist at the University of North Carolina-Greensboro, shows that the death penalty deters more potential homicides than earlier studies had suggested.

Rep. Bill McCollum of Florida says the bill to limit condemned prisoners' habeas corpus appeals "sends the message of swiftness and certainty of punishment that has been missing from our criminal justice system . . . and it goes a long way to restoring deterrence to the criminal justice system." [A habeas corpus appeal allows state and federal inmates to have their cases reviewed by a federal judge, usually after they have lost previous appeals.]

But Leigh Dingerson of the National Coalition to Abolish the Death Penalty says capital punishment has no deterrent effect. "The real implication of [the McCollum] bill is that we'll see cases with significant constitutional error slide through the courts without review," she says. "Most death row inmates were very poorly represented by trial counsel."

That's "the most prominent problem" with the death penalty process, she says. "These are incredibly complex cases at trial, and there just aren't that many attorneys who know how to handle them. So, the more we limit the appeals process, the more we risk executing defendants simply because they had a

Excerpted from "Death Penalty Debate," by Richard L. Worsnop, *CQ Researcher*, March 10, 1995. Reprinted with permission.

lousy lawyer." [The measure to limit habeas corpus appeals was included as part of the Antiterrorism and Effective Death Penalty Act enacted in 1996.]

"In many capital cases," journalist Robert Scheer wrote in the *Los Angeles Times*, "the entire [court] record is less than an inch thick; in some instances, the court-appointed lawyers were drunk and had trouble remembering their clients' names."

Stephen Bright, director of the Atlanta-based Southern Center for Human Rights, holds similar views. "The death penalty is still very arbitrarily inflicted, based primarily on race, poverty, geography and politics," he says. "As a result, it doesn't have much deterrent effect. If you rounded up the 3,000 people who are under death sentence in this country and executed them all today on national television, I doubt that the streets would be any safer tomorrow."

Skepticism About the Death Penalty's Deterrence Effect

According to the recent survey of police chiefs and sheriffs, the death penalty ranks last as a way of reducing violent crime. "Police chiefs would rather spend their limited crime-fighting dollars on such proven measures as community policing, more police training, neighborhood watch programs and long prison sentences," Patrick V. Murphy, former police chief of New York, Washington and Detroit, wrote in *USA Today*.

Some experts argue, in fact, that the death penalty actually encourages homicide in some circumstances. "The threat of capital punishment raises the stakes of getting caught," wrote author Michael Kronenwetter. "Anyone already subject to the death penalty has little to lose by killing again and again. The potential sentence cannot be made any worse than it already is. This makes criminals who already face death for a previous crime more likely to kill in order to avoid being captured . . . to silence any witnesses against them.

> ***"Deterrence is invariably part of the [death-penalty] debate."***

Some psychiatrists, moreover, speculate that homicide occasionally may serve as a roundabout route to suicide. John C. Woods, chief of forensic psychiatry at Utah State Hospital, concluded that Gary Mark Gilmore committed two execution-style murders in Utah because he knew he would face the firing squad. "I think it's a legitimate question . . . to ask if Gilmore would have killed if there was not a death penalty in Utah," said Woods.

Capital Punishment Is a Deterrent

by George E. Pataki

About the author: *George E. Pataki is the Republican governor of New York.*

Sept. 1, 1995, marked the end of a long fight for justice in New York and the beginning of a new era in our state that promises safer communities, fewer victims of crime, and renewed personal freedom. For 22 consecutive years, my predecessors had ignored the urgent calls for justice from our citizens—their repeated and pressing demands for the death penalty in New York State. Even after the legislature passed a reinstatement of the capital punishment law, it was vetoed for 18 years in a row. (Twelve of those vetoes came from the pen of former Gov. Mario Cuomo.)

That was wrong. To fight and deter crime effectively, individuals must have every tool government can afford them, including the death penalty. Upon taking office, I immediately began the process of reinstating the death penalty. Two months later, I signed the death penalty into law for the most heinous and ruthless killers in our society.

A Governmental Priority

Protecting the residents of New York against crime and violence is my first priority. Indeed, it is the most fundamental duty of government. For too long, coddling of criminals allowed unacceptable levels of violence to permeate the streets. They were not subject to swift and certain punishment and, as a result, violent criminal acts were not deterred.

For more than two decades, New York was without the death penalty. During this time, fear of crime was compounded by the fact that, too often, it largely went unpunished.

No more. In New York, the death penalty has turned the tables on fear and put it back where it belongs—in the hearts of criminals. Within just one year, the death penalty helped produce a dramatic drop in violent crime. Just as important, it has restored New Yorkers' confidence in the justice system because they

Reprinted, with permission, from "Death Penalty Is a Deterrent," *USA Today* magazine, March 1997.

know their government genuinely is committed to their safety.

Honest, hard-working people share my vision for a safer New York, a place where children can play outside without worry; parents can send their kids to school with peace of mind; people can turn to each other on any street corner, in any subway, at any hour, without casting a suspicious eye; and New York citizens—of all races, religions, and ages—pull together and stand firm against crime.

> ***"To fight and deter crime effectively, individuals must have every tool government can afford them, including the death penalty."***

In short, we are creating a state where law-abiding citizens have unlimited freedom from crime—a state where all can raise a family and follow their dreams in neighborhoods, streets, and schools that are free from the scourge of crime and violence. We've made tremendous progress. Although the death penalty has contributed to that progress, it's just one facet of New York's broad anti-crime strategy.

Other major reforms include substantially increasing the sentences for all violent criminals; eliminating parole eligibility for virtually all repeat violent offenders; barring murderers and sex offenders from participating in work release programs; toughening penalties for perpetrators of domestic violence; notifying communities as to the whereabouts of convicted sex offenders; overturning court-created criminal-friendly loopholes to make it easier to prosecute violent criminals; and allowing juries to impose a sentence of life without parole for killers.

These new laws are working. Since I took office in 1995, violent crime has dropped 23%, assaults are down 22%, and murders have dropped by nearly one-third. New Yorkers now live in safer communities because we finally have begun to create a climate that protects and empowers our citizens, while giving criminals good cause to fear arrest and conviction. I believe this has occurred in part because of the strong signal that the death penalty and our other tough new laws sent to violent criminals and murderers: You will be punished with the full force of the law.

Shortly before the death penalty went into effect, I listened to the families of 20 murder victims as they told of their pain. No loved ones should have to go through such a wrenching experience. I never will forget the words of Janice Hunter, whose 27-year-old daughter, Adrien, was stabbed 47 times by serial killer Nathaniel White in 1992. Mrs. Hunter spoke for every family member when she said, "It's a heartache that all parents suffer. I have to go to the cemetery to see my daughter. Nathaniel White's mother goes to jail to see him and I don't think it's fair."

Although no law can bring back Mrs. Hunter's daughter, our laws can and must take every responsible step to prevent others from enduring the heartache suffered by her and her family. Before becoming Governor, I supported the death penalty because of my firm conviction that it would act as a significant deterrent and provide a true measure of justice to murder victims and their loved ones.

I know, as do most New Yorkers, that by restoring the death penalty, we have saved lives. Somebody's mother, somebody's brother, somebody's child is alive today because we were strong enough to be tough enough to care enough to do what was necessary to protect the innocent. Preventing a crime from being committed ultimately is more important than punishing criminals after they have shattered innocent lives.

No case illustrates this point more clearly than that of Arthur Shawcross. In 1973, Shawcross, one of New York's most ruthless serial killers, was convicted of the brutal rape and murder of two children in upstate New York. Since the death penalty had been declared unconstitutional, Shawcross was sentenced to prison. After serving just 15 years—an absurd prison term given the crime—he was paroled in 1988. In a horrific 21-month killing spree, Shawcross took 11 more lives. That is 11 innocent people who would be alive today had justice been served in 1973; 11 families that would have been spared the pain and agony of losing a loved one.

By reinstating the death penalty, New York has sent a clear message to criminals that the lives of our children are worth more than just a 15-year prison term. Moreover, it has given prosecutors the legal wherewithal to ensure New York State never has another Arthur Shawcross.

Applying the Ultimate Punishment

Too often, we are confronted with wanton acts of violence that cry out for justice. The World Trade Center bombing and the murderous rampage on the Long Island Rail Road by Colin Ferguson are but two examples. The slaying of a police officer in the line of duty is another. To kill a police officer is to commit an act of war against civilized society.

A person who knowingly commits such a heinous act poses a serious threat to us all, for government cannot protect citizens without doing everything it can to protect those charged with our safety. Police officers put their lives on the line, not knowing whether their next traffic stop or call to duty will be their last.

Under New York's death penalty law, those who murder a police officer; a probation, parole, court, or corrections officer; a judge; or a witness or member of a witness' family can face the death penalty. Someone who murders while already serving life in prison, escaping from prison, or committing other serious felonies can face the death penalty.

> ***"By restoring the death penalty, we have saved lives."***

Contract killers, serial murderers, those who torture their victims, or those who have murdered before also can be sentenced to death. In determining whether the death penalty should be imposed on anyone convicted of first-degree murder, the bill expressly authorizes juries to hear and consider additional evidence whenever the murder was committed as part of an act of terrorism or by someone with two or more prior serious felony convictions.

New York's death penalty is crafted carefully so that only the most inhuman murderers are eligible for it. Upon the conviction of the defendant, a separate sentencing phase is conducted during which the original jury, or a new jury under special circumstances, weighs the facts of the case.

The jury must consider the defendant's prior criminal history, mental capacity, character, background, state of mind, and the extent of his or her participation in the crime. It then compares this evidence with the facts. For the death penalty to be imposed, the jury must reach a verdict unanimously and beyond a reasonable doubt.

Our state lived without adequate protection for 22 years. That is 22 years too long. Now, finally, we have begun to empower New Yorkers with the legal tools they need to make their communities safe.

At the same time, we have put lawless sociopaths like Arthur Shawcross on notice. The time that Shawcross spent in prison was not punishment; it was a mere inconvenience that offered New Yorkers nothing more than a 15-year moratorium from his murderous acts.

Our resolve to end crime is only as strong as the laws we pass to punish criminals. By making the death penalty the law of the land in New York, we have demonstrated that resolve, thus strengthening the promise that our children and future generations will grow up in a state that is free of violence.

The death penalty and the other tough initiatives we have passed are just the beginning of an aggressive and comprehensive plan to reclaim our streets and give New Yorkers back the fundamental freedoms they too often felt had been lost to crime and violence. We will continue to do whatever is necessary to ensure that the lives of New Yorkers are unencumbered by violence, and that is why we will continue to pass laws that give our people unlimited freedom to pursue their hopes and dreams.

Society Needs the Death Penalty to Deter Murderers

by William Tucker

About the author: *William Tucker is the New York correspondent for the* American Spectator, *a conservative monthly periodical.*

Perhaps it is foolish to be optimistic, but the news on crime of late is not all that bad. First and foremost, crime is finally going down. According to FBI statistics, the overall crime index has declined 11 percent since 1991 and is now the lowest it has been since 1985. Violent crimes are at the lowest since 1989. Murders have declined 13 percent since 1991, rape is at its lowest level since 1989, and burglary at the lowest level in two decades. The trend is fairly uniform across the country, with the biggest cities recording the largest drops.

A Dramatic Drop in Crime

At the top of the list is New York City, where crime has plummeted to levels that only a few years ago were unimaginable. Since Mayor Rudy Giuliani took office in 1994, violent crime has fallen an astonishing 40 percent. Murders in New York, which peaked at 2,200 in 1990, fell to 767 in 1997, below the 986 recorded in 1968.

The change of mood in the nation's largest city has been dramatic. Just as crime captured public spaces in the 1960's, leaving the streets to the perpetrators, so a "virtuous cycle" is now returning them to the public. Even at night, public places such as Central Park and the Brooklyn Bridge have become crowded with strollers and passers-by. These well-meaning pedestrians have deprived criminals of their former habitat, serving as a tangible check on crime and disorderly behavior.

All this has been a triumphant confirmation of James Q. Wilson and George Kelling's famous 1982 *Atlantic Monthly* article, "Broken Windows," which has become one of the principal documents of the last half of the twentieth century. Wilson and Kelling argued that public order (what was once called "law and order") was the key to checking violent crime. "If a window in a building is bro-

Excerpted from "Unbroken Windows: The Good News on Crime," by William Tucker, *The American Spectator*, March 1998.

ken and is left unrepaired," they wrote in their now-famous introduction, "all the rest of the windows will soon be broken. One unrepaired broken window is a signal that no one cares, and so breaking more windows costs nothing."

Since the 1960's, the courts had been arguing that laws supporting public order were discriminatory and unconstitutional. In the sixties the Supreme Court overturned statutes against loitering and vagrancy. As late as 1992, the Florida Supreme Court overturned a Tampa ordinance outlawing "loitering for prostitution" on the grounds that the police would be unable to distinguish between prostitutes and wives greeting their husbands. Wilson and Kelling stated the obvious—such prohibitions on maintaining public order are senseless and harmful: "The citizen who fears the ill-smelling drunk, the rowdy teenager, or the importunate beggar is not merely expressing his distaste for unseemly behavior; he is also giving voice to a bit of folk wisdom that happens to be a correct generalization—namely, that serious crime flourishes in areas in which disorderly behavior goes unchecked. The unchecked panhandler is, in effect, the first broken window."

Instead of worrying about maintaining public order, city administrations had become obsessed with fears of police corruption. The remedy was to prevent police interaction with the community. In some cities, patrol officers were not allowed to talk casually with civilians. In New York City, beat officers could not confront street corner drug dealers but had to buck the matter up to special units. As ordinary patrol cars continually drove by congregations of drug dealers without taking any note, neighbors became convinced that the police were corrupt and in the pay of the drug dealers.

The tide finally turned when Mayor Giuliani and Police Commissioner William Bratton, who had been hired by Mayor David Dinkins, started concentrating on "quality of life" crimes. At first there was widespread resistance—even from patrolmen themselves, who had grown used to riding around in patrol cars and ignoring minor problems. But the strategy quickly paid off. "Squeegee men," subway panhandlers, public drunks, and street corner drug dealers were all subject to arrest. Fare-beating had become a major sport on the subways, rising to nearly 50 percent in stations in Harlem and Brownsville. The crackdown produced an added bonus—nearly one in ten fare-beaters was carrying a weapon or wanted on an outstanding warrant. By 1995, fare-beating had been reduced 90 percent.

> ***"It is difficult to have a serious criminal justice system without a death penalty."***

To be sure, there are dissenters. "These things move in cycles, " says Dan Polsby, a professor at Northwestern Law School. "As crime rates have declined recently, people have become more confident about being in public. But this confidence may make them more vulnerable to predation. That would start the cycle on the upswing again." But Kelling is more optimistic. "Just as there's a vicious cycle when good people are driven off the streets by crime and disorderly behavior, so there's a virtuous cycle when they start to reappear again. I think the present gains can be sustained."

But Is the Worst Over?

Beyond the effects of more aggressive policing, however, the outlook dims. What concerns most observers is the demographic bubble of 15- to 30-year-olds that lies just on the horizon. Crimes are committed largely by young men. The problem is that young men—especially minority youth—are getting far more violent. James Fox, dean at Northeastern University, has found that from 1965 to 1985, national homicide rates tracked the proportion of 18- to 24-year-olds in the population almost perfectly. After 1985, the lines separate. There have been far more murders, despite a stagnant youth population. Says David Kopel of the Independence Institute: "The truth is, adult crime rates are now as low as they have been in the last twenty-five years. It's youth crime that is totally out of proportion."

In a 1995 *Atlantic Monthly* article entitled "The Crisis of Public Order," Adam Walinsky, one-time aide to Bobby Kennedy and the nation's foremost advocate of a police corps, blamed this on welfare and crack. "What we experienced from 1985 on was a conjunction of two terrible arrivals. One train carried the legacy of the 1970's, the children of the explosion of illegitimacy and paternal abandonment. Crack arrived on the same timetable, and unloaded at the same station."

> ***"When executions were common in the 1940's and 50's, the murder rate was much lower."***

Nor does he believe the worst is over. "In the year 2000 the black youths born in 1985 will turn fifteen. Three-fifths of them were born to single mothers, many of whom were drug-addicted, one in fourteen will have been raised with neither parent at home; unprecedented numbers have been subject to beatings and other abuse. . . . [N]o matter what efforts we now undertake, we have already assured the creation of more very violent young men than any reasonable society can tolerate."

John DiIulio, Jr., professor of sociology at Princeton and a product of the streets of Philadelphia, is equally pessimistic, also on demographic grounds. He predicts an upsurge of 30,000 to 45,000 murders a year, with other violent offenses rising proportionately. DiIulio has called these youth "superpredators" and attributes their creation to the welfare system and single-parent families. "They do not respond to normal stimuli, have very short time horizons, and absolutely no feeling for their fellow human beings," he says. "They are hardened, remorseless individuals who kill or maim on impulse without any intelligible motive." DiIulio got so sick of encountering these juvenile crime machines in prison settings that he quit interviewing them.

Walinsky would agree. "Social disorder—in its many varieties, and with the assistance of government policies—can perhaps be said to have caused the sudden collapse of family institutions and social bonds that had survived three centuries of slavery and oppression," he wrote in the *Atlantic*. "It is at any rate certain that hundreds of thousands of the children so abandoned have become in turn a major cause of instability. . . . Of all juveniles confined for violent offenses today, less than 30 percent grew up with both parents."

"In America, welfare is now the principal driving force behind crime," says Kopel. "You've got a whole generation of young people who have grown up without fathers. They are reaching the crime-prone age right now. The only positive note for the long term is that welfare reform seems to be going better than anyone expected. A lot will depend on whether black families reform themselves."

Other trends besides welfare reform also promise to turn the tide. [Included] among them . . . [is] the steady return of the death penalty. . . .

The Death Penalty

It is difficult to have a serious criminal justice system without a death penalty. Criminals often testify to the overpowering sense of invulnerability they feel when they attack or kill someone. "I felt like I was indestructible or invincible—like I could just do anything," confessed John Royster, accused of killing a Park Avenue dry cleaner and attacking a Central Park jogger in a 1996 spree. (His lawyers are challenging the admissibility of his statement.) Opponents of the death penalty continue to argue that there is no deterrent to the death penalty, although it is hard to see why. When executions were common in the 1940's and 50's, the murder rate was much lower. When executions stopped in the 1960's, the murder rate took off and did not start coming down until just recently.

The unfortunate custom of racial discrimination has created a controlled experiment in the U.S. over the last half-century. Studies over long periods have shown that the death penalty has been six to ten times less likely to be imposed when the victim was black. In other words, in terms of capital punishment, killing a black is cheap. Not surprisingly, the rate of murder victimization among blacks is five to eight times as high as among whites. There is probably some connection.

One of the most important functions of the law is to distinguish between armed robberies and rapes on the one hand, and murder on the other. Criminals who commit robbery and rape are often tempted to kill their victim in order to eliminate the principal witness. One of the arguments against capital punishment in the 1960's was that 90 percent of murders were "crimes of passion"—the result of arguments among friends or family members. The death penalty, it was argued, could do nothing to prevent these and could be abolished without consequence. Yet the consequence has been that almost half of all homicides are now "stranger murders"—murders committed in the course of other crimes.

These are the murders that had long been deterred by the death penalty. Adam Walinsky notes that, at current clearance rates, the chances a robber will get away with killing his victim are better than 80 percent. "Street thugs may be smarter than they are usually given credit for," says Walinsky.

The good news is that capital punishment is steadily gaining ground. Only thirteen states are now without the death penalty. Executions in 1997 were the highest since 1972—although this was largely because of a high number in one state (Texas). For a while, opponents of the death penalty hoped to confine it to the South and Southwest, thus characterizing it as a yokel phenomenon. But states as diverse as California, Pennsylvania, and Delaware have now held several executions. The endless hand wringing of death-penalty opponents is beginning to ring hollow. Nobody misses Ted Bundy.

In many states, liberals now have their backs to the wall. In October 1997 in Massachusetts, a 10-year-old boy was kidnapped and murdered by two men who had courted him with gifts and were associated with pedophile organizations. The horror of the crime prompted an immediate effort to reinstate the death penalty. Despite 4-to-1 majorities in both houses, Democrats were forced to vote on the issue in December 1997. The measure was about to pass both houses when one liberal Democrat changed his mind, saying he had been influenced by the Louise Woodward case. Republican governor Paul Cellucci promised to make capital punishment the major issue in the following November's legislative elections.

What the legislators and judges fear most about capital punishment is its finality. Yet this is precisely what the public wants. People know that even though some murderer is put in prison on a "life sentence," some future judge or parole board with no familiarity with the case will change their mind and the victims will be dragged through the ordeal all over again. The liberal approach to crime has always underestimated the effect of endless doubt and prevarication on the public mind. Dozens of other social institutions—fire departments, ambulance corps, the police, the military, doctors and hospitals—deal with matters of life and death. If the judges and legislators lack confidence in their own decision-making, why should the public have confidence in them? . . .

"The endless hand wringing of death-penalty opponents is beginning to ring hollow."

[Criminal justice] reforms are obviously not going to happen at once. But there will be incremental change, plus all the indecipherable factors. The courts are a lagging indicator. They like to think of themselves as being smarter than the public—not subject to its "mindless passions"—and are loath to admit they may be following public opinion. But even judges are ultimately responsible to the people they serve.

The truth is, nobody completely understands what causes waves of crime. Looking ahead in 1964, with crime in a steady decline since 1935, anyone might have predicted we were headed toward an unprecedentedly peaceful society. Today, after thirty years of virtual domestic warfare, the past may be no better predictor. Demographics may have their iron law, but until a 16-year-old Dorchester youth was shot last December, there had not been a killing of a juvenile in Boston for twenty-nine months. No one really knows why, but everyone is keeping his fingers crossed.

Executions Reduce the Murder Rate

by George H. Cullins

About the author: *George H. Cullins of Oceanside, California, is the head of Justice Against Crime, an organization that promotes judicial reform.*

As citizens of a society, we must control ourselves, and we must have a deterrent from committing criminal acts. The worst criminal act is the willful and malicious taking of another's life.

The worst crime should have the worst punishment that society can impose, and that is the taking of a murderer's life expeditiously through our court process.

The taking of a life by society, through a court of law, eliminates the personal vendetta and sends a message that society will not tolerate this criminal action.

Society's message is very weak today, when we delay the execution by 15 to 20 years, but the message is there. Ninety-six people who have been on California's death row for 16 years or longer is also a strong message.

In California in 1952, we executed 1½ years after sentencing and the murder rate was 2.4 per 100,000. The rate climbed to 5.4 per 100,000 by 1967, when we stopped executing altogether.

The U.S. Supreme Court stopped all executions in 1976, when the rate had climbed to 10.1 per 100,000. By 1980 the rate climbed to 14.4 per 100,000 when executions started in the United States again. The murder rate in California declined to 10.5 by 1983.

In 1993, after executing Robert Alton Harris in California, the number had reached 12.9 per 100,000. By the time we had executed four, the rate had dropped to 9.0 per 100,000.

In the state of Texas in 1980, when they resumed executions, the rate was 18.0 per 100,000. Now that they have sent a more powerful message, the number is down to 9.0 per 100,000. Houston had 701 murders in 1980, and at last report, it was down to 241 per year. But the message must be stronger if we are to reduce murders further.

Reprinted, with permission, from "Execution Reduces Murders," by George H. Cullins, *North County Times*, November 4, 1998, p. A16.

Execution Saves Lives

Execution saves lives. From 1993 to 1996, the number of murders committed in California has dropped each year. In 1993, 4,095 people were murdered; in 1994 the number dropped to 3,699; in 1995 the number dropped to 3,530 and in 1996 the number dropped to 2,910.

By executing four people, the state saved 1,597 people from being killed in a back alley without judges, juries or the ability to appeal. So in my mind, those who oppose the death penalty would rather see 1,597 people killed in a back alley than execute a murderer after he or she has had a trial by peers, a state appeal process and a federal appeal process.

The only reason to execute anyone is to send a message that society will not tolerate some actions. We must understand that there are those out there who never get the word. The reason to execute is to reduce the murders committed. By executing four people by 1996, the message sent by the society is that if you murder someone in California, your chance of being executed is only .00007. Even with that weak message, it has saved 1,597 families a life of grief.

> ***"With executions, murders drop, and without executions, murders increase."***

Justice Against Crime fights to inform with facts, in the hope of reducing the number of murders committed. We know there will always be murders, but executions reduce the number of murders, if the message is strong enough.

The only reason to execute is to send a message, by society's retributive action, that murders won't be tolerated. With executions, murders drop, and without executions, murders increase. And that's a fact.

Capital Punishment Is Not a Deterrent

by Sean O'Malley

About the author: *Sean O'Malley is a Catholic bishop in Fall River, Massachusetts.*

The Holy Father Pope John Paul II has challenged us to begin the new millennium with a renewed commitment to the Gospel of life. An important way that we can promote the civilization of love in the new millennium is to call for the abolishment of the death penalty. Our task is to work for a more just society and for real solutions to alleviate crime and violence in our communities. The more respect we have for life, the safer our communities will become.

In a growing culture of death, devoid of morality, we face the life-threatening issues such as abortion, immoral genetic practices and experimentation, civil strife, nuclear war, ethnic conflicts, euthanasia and capital punishment. These various assaults on life cannot be melded into a single problem. They are distinct, complicated issues that require individual attention, but they do form pieces of a larger pattern. When human life under any circumstance is not held as sacred in a society, all human life is diminished and threatened.

The church's pro-life stance is consistent and is based on the theological affirmation that the person is made in the image of God, the philosophical assertion of the dignity of every person, and the church's social teaching that society and the state exist to serve the person. Because we hold the sacredness of human life, the taking of even one person's life is a most serious event. Historically, the teaching of the church has allowed the taking of human life only in very rare instances, viz., in the case of self-defense and by extension of this principle, in the case of capital punishment.

It is not surprising that in our own 20th century, the most violent century in recorded history, the presumption on the part of moralists against taking human life has been strengthened and the exceptions deemed ever more restricted. Certainly the dramatic situation with legalized abortion has heightened our aware-

Excerpted from "The Gospel of Life vs. the Death Penalty," by Sean O'Malley, *Origins*, April 1, 1999. Reprinted with permission.

ness of the urgent need to defend the sacredness of every human life.

The Supreme Court in its decision in *Georgia vs. Furman* (1972) held that the death penalty as then administered did constitute cruel and unusual punishment and so was contrary to the Eighth Amendment of the Constitution. In *Gregg vs. Georgia* in 1976 the court allowed states to resume using the death penalty. This decision claimed that new procedures would address the objections involved in the previous ruling and so set off the debate once again. Since that time, many people have been surprised that the bishops' conference has consistently opposed the death penalty, in spite of the contrary opinion of a majority of Catholics in the United States. However, Catholic teachings are not based on polls or prevailing sentiments, but upon the magisterium with the twofold font of Scripture and tradition.

"The more respect we have for life, the safer our communities will become."

The Myth of Deterrence

Since the popularity of the death penalty in great part issues from people's frustration over violent crimes, one of the most popular arguments in favor of the death penalty is its presumed value as a deterrent. The conventional wisdom is that we need capital punishment to discourage people from committing murder. Politicians often appeal to the deterrence factor as a justification of the death penalty. When Gov. George Pataki signed legislation that reinstated the death penalty in New York in 1995, he stated, "This bill is going to save lives." Former Gov. William Weld, in his attempts to reinstate the death penalty in Massachusetts, said, "My gut is that . . . capital punishment is a deterrent." Nevertheless, more scientific approaches seem to indicate that capital punishment is not a deterrent.

A survey authored by Richard C. Dieter that was conducted in 1995 involving interviews with 386 randomly selected police chiefs and sheriffs resulted in only 1 percent of the respondents choosing the death penalty as a primary way to reduce violent crime. The death penalty ranked last among six options. The most effective way named by the police chiefs and sheriffs was "reducing drug abuse," followed by "better economy and more jobs."

Simplifying court rules, longer sentences, more police officers and reducing the number of guns were also considered to be more important as ways of reducing violent crimes than expanding the use of the death penalty. Of those interviewed, 67 percent termed inaccurate the statement, "The death penalty significantly reduces the number of homicides."

Commenting on the poll, former New York Police Chief Patrick Murphy wrote: "Like the emperor's new clothes, the flimsy notion that the death penalty is an effective law enforcement tool is being exposed as mere political puffery."

A similar survey by Michael Radelet and Ronald Akers among the leadership of the country's largest associations of professional and academic criminologists such as the American Society of Criminology (2,500 members) and the International Association of Police Professors (membership 2,400) likewise debunks the deterrent benefits of the death penalty. Of the experts interviewed, 80 percent stated that on the basis of literature and research in criminology the death penalty does not have significant deterrent effects.

It would seem that the best deterrence is crime prevention and dealing with the causes and situations such as poverty and drug addiction that foment crime and violence.

For any punishment to be an effective deterrence, it must be administered fairly and swiftly. Experience has shown how difficult it is to administer capital punishment "fairly and swiftly." When someone is accused of a crime, if he is poor or of a minority group he is more likely to be condemned to death than someone who is wealthy and well-educated.

The delays and costs involved in appeals and other necessary procedural safeguards make it impossible to execute criminals swiftly. Short of a reign of terror, one is hard pressed to conceive how the death penalty could be administered in such a way that it would become an effective deterrent. It would be much more feasible to improve court proceedings and bring about swifter justice if the maximum punishment would be incarceration without parole.

> ***"Experts . . . stated that on the basis of literature and research in criminology the death penalty does not have significant deterrent effects."***

Allowing months and even years to pass between the time of the arrest and the imposition of a punishment certainly undermines the deterrence value of any sentencing. In addition to vitiating any value as a deterrent, the prolonged proceedings of capital punishment subject the families of victims to tortuous years of criminal hearings and appeals, often preventing healing and closure in their lives. Expeditious trials and life sentences without parole for heinous crimes would be more merciful not only to the criminals but also to the families of the victims. . . .

Within the United States, one-third of the states have already abolished capital punishment. The opposition to the death penalty is widespread and diverse. Catholic, Protestant and Jewish groups as well as many national organizations have expressed their opposition based on religious, moral and civic reasons.

As we prepare to end the most violent century in the history of the world and as we cross the threshold of hope into a new millennium, we must join our voices with that of our Holy Father in calling for an abolition of the death penalty. We want our country to be characterized by justice, not revenge; by safety, not violence; by life, not death.

Capital Punishment May Cause Violence to Increase

by Philip Brasfield

About the author: *Philip Brasfield is a contributing editor for* The Other Side, *a bimonthly nondenominational Christian journal. He has been in prison for more than twenty years.*

> It is the deed that teaches, not the name we give it. Murder and capital punishment are not opposites that cancel one another but similars that breed their kind.
>
> —George Bernard Shaw

The rash of violent crimes committed in the past year by juveniles has shocked the nation. Our alarm increases with each new report of the location, body count, and young ages of the children involved.

The entire nation was horrified in the spring of 1998 when two boys aged twelve and fourteen opened fire on their schoolmates in Jonesboro, Arkansas, killing a teacher and four students and wounding ten other students. Similar episodes have unfolded in 1998 in Mississippi, Oregon, and Kentucky. The tremors created by these crimes have shaken us all, including those of us locked away here in this Texas prison.

We are all left struggling to comprehend the rage that underlies such crimes. What would motivate seemingly normal children to perpetrate such violence?

Given the shock and anger surrounding these crimes, it's not surprising that in Texas (the death-penalty capital of the Western world) a legislator has proposed a new crime bill that would lower the age at which one can be executed to eleven years old. Representative Jim Pitts, himself the father of a fifth-grader, claims his office received hundreds of phone calls after he introduced the bill: "About 60 percent in favor and 40 percent against." Referring to the many supporters of the bill, Pitts comments, "These are not the 'Leave It to Beaver' types I grew up with."

I suppose a lot of folks in and out of prison have been battered beyond the healing honesty of tears. The voices on talk radio argue more about the age at

Reprinted, with permission, from "The Deed That Teaches," by Philip Brasfield, *The Other Side*, November/December 1998.

which kids reach moral and legal responsibility for their action than about why we continue to arm ourselves more than any other Western country. Have we convinced ourselves that we are immune to the inevitable backlash of violence against others throughout our history?

Charlie Rumbaugh was one of the first friends I made on death row, and the first "juvenile offender" I knew who was condemned to die. A reform-school runaway, he'd robbed and killed an aging jeweler in Amarillo. Because of his violent past in the juvenile system, Charlie was tried as an adult—and sentenced to death.

"Many studies . . . have noted* increases *in murder rates in the months following an execution."

Charlie was the first one to tell you he was guilty—and that he knew exactly what *guilty* meant. For most of us, *guilty* is a word used to justify blame. But *guilty* is also a feeling of immense weight, a spiritual burden that grows heavier with time. Charlie carried that burden throughout his time in prison.

As almost always happens, the man that Charlie Rumbaugh became while waiting to be executed was a far cry from the scared, dumb runaway who shot and killed another human. In prison, confronting the realities of life and death, he became a better person than he'd ever thought possible. His execution several years ago ended his dream of working to help the kind of kids he'd once been.

The Death Penalty Acquires a Human Face

Support for the death penalty has always been high here in Texas—around 70 percent. But in the aftermath of Karla Faye Tucker's execution in 1998, surveys revealed that the number of folks supporting the death penalty had dropped by more than 20 percent. Tucker's highly publicized case, and the days leading up to her execution, had given the death penalty a human face.

Tucker was a teenager when she participated in a pair of horrific and brutal murders. On death row, she confronted her own deep outrage and sorrow over her actions, and the shattering reality of how deeply human evil can reside in one's life. Christianity enabled her to make sense of her life and led her to become a different person.

Karla Faye Tucker lived her faith in prison, and it showed. She knew she could never change the fact that she had hacked two people to death with a pickaxe, but her faith assured her that she had been redeemed from the darkest depths and now lived "in the light."

Tucker's situation was hotly debated behind these walls, just as it was outside them. Many here believed Texas would never execute a woman. Others thought Texas governor George Bush might pardon her, because she was Christian—or maybe because he's one, too. Still others placed hope in the Board of Pardons and Paroles, even though it has never, since the reinstatement of the death penalty in 1972, commuted a death sentence based solely upon the petition of the condemned.

I argued all along that if ever Texas *had* to execute someone, it was Karla Faye. Failure to execute her because of her gender or religious faith would have opened the door to litigation from hundreds of male prisoners, including the many men on death row who claim a born-again faith in Christ. In the end, despite the outcry of religious leaders like Pat Robertson and Pope John Paul II, as well as thousands of plain folks, Karla Faye Tucker died for her sins.

Of the 447 people on Texas's death row as I write this, twenty-seven were juveniles when convicted of murder. At the beginning of 1998, sixty-seven persons nationwide were awaiting execution for murders committed as juveniles. Many states continue to aggressively extend their use of the death penalty to cover more cases and younger ages, without any evidence that such measures will reduce the violence.

In light of the many studies that have noted *increases* in murder rates in the months following an execution, we have to wonder what kind of message our nation's willingness to kill its own citizens—even its children—is sending to our young people. As Michael Godfrey of the Center on Juvenile and Criminal Justice wrote in a recent study, "The state may be tragically leading by example."

"We have to wonder what kind of message our nation's willingness to kill its own citizens—even its children—is sending to our young people."

Could this be so? Are the kids in Arkansas and Kentucky and Oregon and the rest of America watching what we allow the state to do in our names and following our tragic example? When the state takes a person out of a cage where it has held them for years and kills them "to solve a problem" are the kids brutalized—even if the rest of society is too distracted or apathetic to notice?

If we are serious about reducing crime and violence in our country, then killing the death penalty is a place to begin. By ending, rather than expanding, the state-sanctioned violence of executions, we will teach our children to truly value all life.

Chapter 4

Should Capital Punishment Be Abolished?

Chapter Preface

In a recent survey that asked "Do you favor or oppose the death penalty for persons convicted of murder?" 75 percent of Americans responded in favor of capital punishment, according to researcher R.M. Bohm. However, a U.S. Justice Department study reveals that when people are given information about several specific crimes that are punishable by execution, a majority will choose long prison terms over the death penalty.

This news has raised the hopes of opponents of capital punishment, who often argue that murderers should receive life sentences rather than death sentences. As punishment for the crime of first-degree murder, many states permit life sentences that strictly limit the possibility of parole; at least eighteen states allow life sentences with no possibility of parole. Richard Dieter, executive director of the Death Penalty Information Center, contends that the number of death sentences in a state tends to decrease after the passage of laws allowing the alternative of life without parole. "When juries have a choice," says Dieter, "they are picking [life without parole] as a middle ground." Death penalty critics argue that juries' preference for the sentence of life without parole reveals a popular desire to avoid the execution of innocent people. Moreover, Dieter adds, "What people want is safety. And they want punishment. Life without parole gives them that."

Supporters of the death penalty, on the other hand, maintain that the sentence of life without parole guarantees neither safety nor punishment. For one thing, proponents contend, a dangerous murderer serving a life sentence can escape from prison and kill again. State sentencing laws can also change over a period of years, possibly allowing the release of convicts who had originally been sentenced to life. Furthermore, argues nationally syndicated columnist Don Feder, life imprisonment is a sorely inadequate punishment for the crime of deliberate murder: "Lifers aren't exactly living the life of Reilly. Still, they live. Even in the harshest of [penal institutions], there are opportunities to laugh, form friendships, read, be entertained, learn, communicate, even love—emotions and experiences forever denied to [murder victims]." To increase public safety and to ensure that murderers receive a punishment befitting their crime, Feder and capital-punishment supporters promote the death penalty rather than life sentences without parole.

Capital-punishment alternatives and reforms continue to provoke intense debate among lawmakers, criminal justice experts, theologians, and the general public. The authors of the following chapter offer various opinions on this much-discussed topic.

The Death Penalty Should Be Abolished

by Helen Prejean, interviewed by Vicki Quade

About the author: *Helen Prejean is a Catholic nun in the order of the Sisters of St. Joseph of Medaille. She is also an anti-death penalty activist and the author of* Dead Man Walking. *Prejean is interviewed by Vicki Quade, an editor of the quarterly journal* Human Rights.

Vicki Quade: We are taught that life is sacred, yet the people you deal with don't believe that.

Helen Prejean: We are taught in the American way of life that some life is sacred. Innocent life is sacred. I don't know that we've ever been taught that guilty life is sacred.

I don't think we've been taught justice even in the ways that our laws are enacted. We have always been taught that some life is more sacred than other life.

When it comes to criminal law and criminal justice, you can definitely see that who the victim is and the status of the victim propels and initiates the justice and the punishment that is sought.

There is a direct correlation.

The more we identify with the person killed, the more outrage that is felt over the death. When other people are killed we don't identify with, there doesn't seem to be all that passion and outrage over the death.

There is a discrepancy.

We know what the fault lines are. We know that race has a lot to do with it. When white people are killed, when people have certain status, when a law professor or a policeman is killed, people are more outraged and punishment is more vigorously pursued.

So when we learn that all life is sacred, well, right away when you see the punishment given, you can see some life must be more sacred than other life.

Our society assumes that some people are so evil, it's okay for our government to execute them. But you think that basic assumption is wrong.

Yes, any more than you can say that somebody is so totally good, they're a saint.

That's what they're trying to do to me now. They're trying to make me into a saint. Maybe it's because labels save us time. They're a shorthand in trying to deal with people who are always complex, and who always pop out of the boxes we put them into.

> ***"You can selectively quote from scripture until the cows come home. Here's where God said kill for adultery. . . . Here's where God said kill a whole village. Want to do that?"***

We do that with both good and evil. Like Mother Teresa. You know we will attribute nothing bad to her.

Then, when somebody has done a terrible thing, we say that's all there is to them. When I'm talking with audiences, I'll say: Suppose there was a way that the worst thing you had ever done could be projected on a screen for everybody to see.

Then suppose you were told, "That is all you are."

You'd say, "I've been kind to my grandmother. I was honest on my test in school."

We can never transfix into one single, absolute category any human being. That's the simplistic kind of shorthand that politicians love to use. They do that with the death penalty as a solution to crime.

Selective Scripture Quoting

Politicians look at the Bible and say, God kills. They talk about Sodom and Gomorrah. Or the Great Flood. They can make the argument that God believes that people are inherently evil and should be disposed of, so why shouldn't government.

That's right. Follow that through and read through the Bible.

Even when the Israelites came into what they called the promised land, the land of Canaan, you hear coming from God's mouth, "When you go to take those villages, kill every man, woman, and child, and all the animals."

There's a lot of killing coming from the mouth of God.

But remember, the Bible was written over a 2,000-year period. It's a testimony of the religious experience of people over 2,000 years, but you definitely see a progression as you move along in the Bible.

In primitive days, where there were no institutions, no prisons, no alternative ways where society could incapacitate violent people, you see harsh, swift punishment.

The death penalty was applied for many, many things.

Interestingly, when people quote the Bible, they never say, "Look at the death penalty for adultery." That's from the mouth of God, too. Should we go back now to killing one another for adultery?

It's a very selective process in quoting from the scriptures. What I've discovered is everybody wants God in their corner.

As far as lawyers or prosecutors go, I've witnessed that with the head of the district attorney for Louisiana. When we appeared before the judicial committee of the Louisiana legislature about the death penalty, he came armed, not with legal text, but with quotes from scripture.

Everybody wants to have the ultimate authority in their corner.

But you can selectively quote from scripture until the cows come home. Here's where God said kill for adultery. Want to do that? Here's where God said kill a whole village. Want to do that?

People know. Instinctively they know that was from another era, from another time. Definitely the progression in the scripture, even by the time you get to the later prophets of Ezekiel and Jeremiah and Isaiah, is towards compassion.

More and more it's not to imitate the hatred and the violence. And then, when you get into the New Testament and into the life and example of Jesus, there is that, "not to humiliate the enemy, not to return hate for hate."

Changing Society's Opinion

Are you trying to change society's opinion of these killers?

I'm trying to change society's opinion about whether the government has the right to kill these killers.

What I'm trying to change is, yes, people do despicable things, people do heinous things at which all decent people are outraged.

But now—and here's the key moral question—not what do we do with the innocent people, but what do we do with people who are truly guilty of heinous crimes? And then when you start really looking at it, who are the human agents to whom we will entrust the bringing of justice or giving of justice, supposing that we could even mandate them with that decision over life and death.

Nobody more than lawyers knows the frailty of our legal system for getting justice in this country. Even about collecting back taxes or over a lawsuit, much less over the decision of putting someone to death or letting them live.

"Definitely the progression in the scripture . . . is towards compassion. More and more it's not to imitate the hatred and the violence."

Do you think we'll ever eliminate the death penalty?

Yeah, eventually we will. It'll come about because it may be that it'll just be too costly for us. And costliness is not just in the money, but it will be when people realize that, well, it might even come that it's too complex in the courts.

The Supreme Court justices in California and Florida are objecting that over half of their court time is in reviewing capital cases.

What if they made the amount of time involved shorter?

It's complex to get all the mitigating circumstances, to get all the aggravating circumstances, to do it through a trial, through an appeal. It's complex.

It's almost like the rhetoric is very simplistic, but the law is complex.

What if the law was streamlined to make it easier?

Then we'd be doing away with people's constitutional rights. In order to streamline it, we'd have to say that death is no different than any other law, let's line 'em up, go in the back yard, and the whole thing can be over in a month.

If you build that kind of simplicity into the process of law over something as serious as life and death, then their human rights, their civil rights will be curtailed. Their constitutional rights will necessarily be curtailed.

Basic Human Rights

Are there any laws on the books today that might help to abolish the death penalty?

The Universal Declaration of Human Rights of the United Nations, which states that everybody, no matter what they have done has certain basic human rights that are non-negotiable, that governments don't give for good behavior or take away for bad behavior.

And those two basic human rights are not to be tortured, and not to be killed.

Torture is intrinsic to the death penalty. And we can argue about how much torture there is to the electric chair, or gas chamber, or even lethal injections, about what people feel physically.

> ***"[The] two basic human rights are not to be tortured, and not to be killed."***

But I can witness, in fact, that people have died a thousand times mentally before they've died physically. You can't condemn a person to death and not have them anticipate their death, imagine their death, and vicariously experience their death many, many times before they die.

Every one of the men I've accompanied have all had the same nightmare. They can control their conscious thoughts, but they can't control them in sleep. The same nightmare is they're coming to get me, the guards are holding me down, the execution chamber, I'm fighting, I'm sweating, and I'm yelling, "No, no."

If we can acknowledge that brainwashing is a form of torture, then how long will it take us to acknowledge that sentencing conscious human beings to their death is a form of torture.

Then you add to that process that when you go into the death house to die and there are those two telephones on the wall—one to the courts and one to the governor—and when that phone rings and you get a stay, you begin that process all over again.

It's being on that tightwire, between life and death, being prepared for either is an incredible torture for people.

What is the appropriate punishment for acts of inhuman violence?

Serious crimes call for serious punishment. The most serious crime calls for the most serious punishment, and that translates in our modern society as long-term imprisonment.

Over the last 10 years, many state legislatures have tightened up sentencing for first degree murder. People are not getting out after a few, short years.

The alternate to death is life.

Many states have life without parole, or mandatory long-term imprisonment before which the person can be considered for parole.

How do you answer those who say the death penalty is just? It's not being done for retribution, but for justice.

Justice is a euphemism for revenge. And when they say it's for justice, I say, "For whom?"

> ***"If . . . brainwashing is a form of torture, then how long will it take us to acknowledge that sentencing conscious human beings to their death is a form of torture."***

And they say, "Well the people, the community, the victims' family."

But if you notice, what moved the initiative that brought back the death penalty was not from victims' families across this country calling for the death penalty. They ain't never been the ones. It's been politicians who have initiated the death penalty back into existence.

The mood in Congress is to eliminate habeas corpus, which responds to our country's desire for retribution. How can you buck that kind of system?

To eliminate habeas is another way to be hard on criminals.

The three targets in Congress now are immigrants, poor (especially welfare recipients), and criminals.

This is part of that wave of chain gangs for criminals, long sentences for criminals, executions for criminals, doing away with "too many rights" for criminals, habeas corpus being one of them.

That just shows the shrillness and mean-spiritedness of it. Of course, criminals are easy targets for politicians. They're not exactly going to lose a lot of votes if they come down hard on criminals.

Criminals can't vote. People who have been in prison can't vote. And so they're easy targets to get.

You've done a lot for the image of nuns, but you don't sing, you don't fly.

I sing, I do. And I fly a lot on airplanes!

What kind of image do you think you project?

A dedicated life who makes her faith work for justice. Who stands on the side of poor and struggling people and tries to bring the love of God, or love from faith to the transformation of society.

It's an unnerving kind of ministry, isn't it?

You mean, watching people get executed? Why sure, that's definitely unnerving. And being with victims' families is unnerving.

Being with people who have experienced such a radical loss in their lives, such radical pain, is unnerving.

How were you drawn to that?

The simple, direct answer to how I got involved with death row inmates is 'cause I got involved with poor people. It's a greased track, at least in Louisiana, of being poor and being on death row.

So our community, the Sisters of St. Joseph of Medaille, made a decision in 1980 that we were going to stand on the side of poor people and get involved in social justice, making our faith work for justice.

Lo and behold, man, it was a greased track. I got involved with poor people and, blunk, there we were: "Hey, you want to write to somebody on death row?" Sure, I knew the person was poor, and it was part of my work with the poor.

It all escalated from there.

Why don't more people do the kind of work you do?

More and more people are doing the kind of work I do. The religious women in the Catholic Church have always been the ones in the trenches, in the homeless shelters, AIDS shelters. 'Cause that's our job, to comfort, to serve, to help people get out from injustice and live human, decent lives.

In fact, the Leadership Conference of Religious Women sent out a press release on the film [*Dead Man Walking*]. Of course, they're happy about the image of sisters for the first time. You don't have a nun running off with somebody, or flying, like you said.

They indicated in there that 40 percent of women religious in the U.S. today are, in one way or another, in touch with people in prison. That's where poor people are. That's where struggling people are.

We incarcerate 1.3 million in this country, more than any other country in the world except Russia. This is where a lot of poor and struggling people are.

Going back to the gospels of Jesus. Just who was Jesus with? You find that he gravitated toward and was in the company of people who were considered the throwaways of society. Sisters do the same.

The Death Penalty Should Be Retained

by Justice for All

About the author: *Justice for All is a criminal justice reform organization dedicated to protecting citizens from violent crime.*

Although not relevant to the legal application of the death penalty in the United States, religious issues are a significant thread within the moral debate. Biblical text is most relevant within a theocracy or a secular government which has laws that are consistent with biblical text. The United States does not, of course, fall within either category. This viewpoint is included only to counter the false claim that there is no New Testament support for capital punishment.

The Bible Does Not Prohibit the Death Penalty

• Virtually all religious scholars agree that the correctly translated commandment "Thou shalt not murder" is a prohibition against individual cases of murder. There is no biblical prohibition against the government imposition of the death penalty in deserving cases. Indeed, the government imposition of capital punishment is required for deliberate murder. . . .

• According to Clark University philosophy professor Michael Pakaluk, "If no crime deserves the death penalty, then it is hard to see why it was fitting that Christ be put to death for our sins and crucified among thieves. St. Thomas Aquinas quotes a gloss of St. Jerome on Matthew 27: 'As Christ became accursed of the cross for us, for our salvation He was crucified as a guilty one among the guilty.' That Christ be put to death as a guilty person, presupposes that death is a fitting punishment for those who are guilty.". . .

• Carl F.H. Henry, author of *Twilight of a Great Civilization*, contends that "The rejection of capital punishment is not to be dignified as a 'higher Christian way' that enthrones the ethics of Jesus. The argument that Jesus as the incarnation of divine love cancels the appropriateness of capital punishment in the New Testament era has little to commend it. Nowhere does the Bible repudiate capital punishment for premeditated murder; not only is the death penalty for

Excerpted from "Death Penalty and Sentencing Information in the United States," by Justice for All, October 1, 1997. Reprinted with permission.

deliberate killing of a fellow human being permitted, but it is approved and encouraged, and for any government that attaches at least as much value to the life of an innocent victim as to a deliberate murderer, it is ethically imperative.". . .

• St. Thomas Aquinas finds all biblical interpretations against executions "frivolous," citing Exodus 22:18, "wrongdoers thou shalt not suffer to live." Unequivocally, he states, "The civil rulers execute, justly and sinlessly, pestiferous men in order to protect the peace of the state."

• According to Protestant scholar Reuben Hahn, "God, Himself, instituted the death penalty (Genesis 9:6) and Christ regarded capital punishment as a just penalty for murder (Matthew 26:52). God gave to government the legitimate authority to use capital punishment to restrain murder and to punish murderers. Not to inflict the death penalty is a flagrant disregard for God's divine Law which recognizes the dignity of human life as a product of God's creation. Life is sacred, and that is why God instituted the death penalty. Consequently, whoever takes innocent human life forfeits his own right to live."

• In Book III of *Summa Contra Gentiles*, Aquinas states: "The fact that the evil, as long as they live, can be corrected from their errors does not prohibit the fact that they may be justly executed, for the danger which threatens from their way of life is greater and more certain than the good which may be expected from their improvement. They also have at that critical point of death the opportunity to be converted to God through repentance. And if they are so stubborn that even at the point of death their heart does not draw back from evil, it is possible to make a highly probable judgement that they would never come away from evil to the right use of their powers."

Punishment and Redemption

• The movie *Dead Man Walking* reveals a perfect example of how just punishment and redemption can work together. Had rapist/murderer Matthew Poncelet not been properly sentenced to death by the civil authority, he would not have met Sister Helen Prejean, he would not have received spiritual instruction, he would not have taken responsibility for his crimes and he would not have reconciled with God. Had Poncelet never been caught or had he only been given a prison sentence, his character makes it VERY clear that those elements would not have come together. Indeed, for the entire film and up until those last moments, prior to his execution, Poncelet was not fully truthful with Sister Prejean. His lying and manipulative nature was fully exposed at that crucial time. It was not at all surprising, then, that it was just prior to his execution that all of the spiritual elements may have come together for his salvation. It was now, or never. Truly, just as St. Aquinas predicted, it was his

"There is no biblical prohibition against the government imposition of the death penalty in deserving cases."

pending execution which finally led to his repentance. For Christians, the most crucial concerns of *Dead Man Walking* must be and are redemption and eternal salvation. And, for that reason, it may well be, for Christians, the most important pro–death penalty movie ever made.

> ***"We should err on the side of caution and not give murderers the opportunity to harm again."***

A real life example of this may be the case of Dennis Gentry, executed April 16, 1997, for the highly premeditated murder of his friend Jimmy Don Ham. During his final statement, Gentry said, "I'd like to thank the Lord for the past 14 years (on death row) to grow as a man and mature enough to accept what's happening here tonight. To my family, I'm happy. I'm going home to Jesus." As the lethal drugs began to flow, Gentry cried out, "Sweet Jesus, here I come. Take me home. I'm going that way to see the Lord." We cannot know if Gentry or the fictitious Poncelet or the two real murderers from the book *Dead Man Walking* really did repent and receive salvation. But, we do know that St. Aquinas advises us that murderers should not be given the benefit of the doubt. We should err on the side of caution and not give murderers the opportunity to harm again. Indeed, as Dr. W.H. Baker confirms in his *On Capital Punishment*, biblical text finds that it is a violation of God's mandate not to execute premeditated murderers—and nowhere does the text contradict this finding.

Capital Punishment Should Not Be Applied Unless Absolutely Necessary

by Renato Martino

About the author: *Archbishop Renato Martino is the Vatican's official emissary to the United Nations. The following viewpoint is taken from an address he presented on February 5, 1999, to the New York University law school.*

It is my pleasure to be with you today at New York University as we address the important—and controversial—subject of the death penalty. The issue is a hotly debated one on the international scene, particularly at U.N. headquarters, where one hears more and more from nations a call to abandon its practice, if not its total abolition.

Very recently, during the Holy Father's [1999] visit to St. Louis, Mo., he renewed his appeal made a month earlier for a consensus to end the death penalty, calling it "both cruel and unnecessary" (from the Jan. 27, 1999, homily). At a more grass-roots level, we are increasingly hearing of pleas by individuals and groups who are realizing that fighting violence with violence does not achieve a useful purpose in society nor does it allow us to foster an ethic of respect of life that moves beyond vengeance in order to deal with violence in a more effective way.

What I share with you today is nothing new—I have spoken on this topic before. My presentation today, however, is a more detailed explication of those views. I do realize that the death penalty is a sensitive and heated topic. And so we must not relegate it to theoretical, ivory-tower discussions, as it involves not only criminals but victims who have truly been violated, their families and friends, and indeed, our very society as well.

Anger and Frustration at Rampant Crime

Media accounts are daily filled with stories of senseless violence, oftentimes against innocent people: the rape and murder of a child snatched from a school-

Reprinted, with permission, from "The United Nations and the Death Penalty," by Renato Martino, *Origins*, March 18, 1999.

yard; a young woman beaten and raped while strolling in a park; the killing of an elderly couple in the comfort of their home; a baby left for dead in a dumpster only minutes after his birth. Respectable people instinctively recoil at such horrors, wondering when—and if—the violence will ever cease. They look into the innocent faces and trusting eyes of their young children and grandchildren, concerned over how best to protect them. They fear for the elderly, knowing that there are some people who, in the blink of an eye, would take advantage of them for their own selfish gain. And the result—society becomes filled with fear and cries out for a deterrent. And should that deterrent fail to eliminate future crime, at least vengeance has been brought to the perpetrator.

"Fighting violence with violence does not achieve a useful purpose in society."

Oftentimes it is the lack of remorse by many criminals that encourages good people to support the death penalty. Even among Catholics, a 1997 Gallup Poll found that 51 percent believed that the death penalty should be the punishment for murder, while 43 percent felt that the punishment should be life imprisonment with no chance for parole. Is this majority—however narrow—a reflection of the anger and frustration with the crime and violence that are destroying our society?

Actually, capital punishment falls within the boundaries of legitimate defense. Those who support it claim that it restores the dignity and value of the victim whose life was taken in a violent way. They say that if one person is willing to take another's life, he ought to be willing to pay for it as well. He has a debt to pay to society, and law and order must be maintained.

Specifically, those in favor of capital punishment put forward three arguments: a) It is a deterrent to crime by instilling fear in anyone who might consider doing likewise; b) it is a comfort to the families of murder victims, since it exacts upon the criminal the same wrongfulness he enacted upon his victim; and c) it protects society by eliminating a "cancer" from it, once and for all.

Refuting the Arguments

However, a closer look at these arguments reveals some terrible flaws. While capital punishment certainly prevents the individual criminal from committing further crimes, it has not proven to be an effective deterrent to crime in general. It is naive to believe that a murderer takes time to reflect upon the consequences of his or her crime, even should that consequence be his or her own execution. Also, we have seen that countries which advocate the death penalty have murder rates that are as high, if not higher, than those which do not support it.

We must ask ourselves, Does killing the criminal honor the victim? Does it enhance the lives of a victim's family? Is it a constructive or appropriate method of dealing with the anger? No. I recall one woman who, regarding the criminal convicted of killing one of her family members, said, "I don't believe that killing him is going to make my loss any less." In that statement this insightful woman acknowledges the reality that executing the criminal will not bring back a loved one nor will it take away the pain.

This leaves us, then, with the need to protect society. In this regard, however, we must ask, If criminals can remain in jail forever, do we really need to bloody our own hands by joining in the killing? I once read a statement that summarized the matter quite succinctly with a question: "Why do we kill people who killed people, to show that killing is wrong?" In reality, would not life imprisonment without the possibility of parole satisfy the need to protect society?

Another important issue to consider is the fact that innocent persons will continue to be falsely accused and executed for crimes they did not commit. But at least an innocent person serving a life sentence still has the possibility of one day being proven innocent. To my knowledge, in all of human history only one innocent man who was unjustly executed was ever resurrected. That hasn't happened again in the past 2,000 years. Once the death penalty has been enacted, it can never be retracted.

Church Teaching

There are many misconceptions regarding the position of the Catholic Church on the issue of capital punishment. Many state—and accurately—that the church has never absolutely banned the death penalty. Proponents often quote the Old Testament: "life for life, eye for eye, tooth for tooth, hand for hand" (Ex. 21:23-24). What is not clearly understood is that this passage refers not so much to sanction stern penalties, but to protect individuals from excessive punishments such as those that are cruel, unreasonable and ineffective.

Those who advocate "eye for eye, tooth for tooth" oftentimes fail to heed three other important passages. In Genesis (4:15) God ensures that death will not be inflicted upon Cain, who has killed his brother Abel. In this passage, God says: "'If anyone kills Cain, Cain shall be avenged sevenfold.' So the Lord put a mark on Cain, lest anyone should kill him at sight." In Ezekiel (33:11) we read, "As I live, says the Lord God, I swear I take no pleasure in the death of the wicked man, but rather in the wicked man's conversion, that he may live." In the Sermon on the Mount of the New Testament Scriptures, Christ exhorts: "You have heard that it was said, 'An eye for an eye and a tooth for a tooth.' But I say to you not to resist the evildoer; on the contrary, if someone strikes you on the right cheek, turn to him and offer the left as well" (Mt. 5:38-39).

"One cannot teach—as the Fifth Commandment states—that killing is wrong while repeating unnecessarily the same dreadful act that the criminal has committed."

Turning back for a moment to the Genesis account of Cain, we must understand that in sparing Cain's life God does not leave his crime unpunished. While God rejects the enactment of capital punishment upon Cain, he does render justice. Cain, in essence, receives a life sentence without parole. He is cursed by God and also by the earth, which will deny him its fruit. He receives a sentence of loneliness and separation from God, a sentence that will be with him forever.

One cannot teach—as the Fifth Commandment states—that killing is wrong while repeating unnecessarily the same dreadful act that the criminal has committed. Each and every human life is created in the image and likeness of God. Even the murderer, in spite of his or her cruel deed, does not lose personal dignity.

Pope John Paul II, in his 1995 encyclical letter *Evangelium Vitae*, says: "And it is precisely here that the paradoxical mystery of the merciful justice of God is shown forth. . . . God, who preferred the correction rather than the death of a sinner, did not desire that a homicide be punished by the exaction of another act of homicide" (No. 9). Thus society, in punishing the criminal, must aim and hope for the rehabilitation of the criminal.

The Catechism of the Catholic Church, released in 1992, takes justice into account when dealing with the issue of capital punishment and the right of public authorities to punish criminals with penalties commensurate with the crime. It reminds us of the importance of considering public safety and the loss suffered by a family. But it also teaches that the punishment must redress the offense as well as contribute to the rehabilitation of the offender.

While "preserving the common good of society requires rendering the aggressor unable to inflict harm," it follows that "if bloodless means are sufficient to defend human lives . . . public authority should limit itself to such means, because they better correspond to the concrete conditions of the common good and are more in conformity to the dignity of the human person."

Developments in Church Teaching

Evangelium Vitae affirms the catechism's teaching but takes it even further by enumerating conditions under which it would be morally acceptable. Given the development of most penal systems in our day, the Holy Father states that the nature and extent of punishment "ought not go to the extreme of executing the offender except in cases of absolute necessity: in other words, when it would not be possible otherwise to defend society." Then, he adds, "Today however, as a result of steady improvements in the organization of the penal system, such cases are rare, if not practically nonexistent."

While affirming the principle set forth in the Catechism of the Catholic Church regarding the use of bloodless means, *Evangelium Vitae*, released only three years after the catechism, would necessitate an adjustment of the catechism's language on this subject. Thus, on Sept. 9, 1997, among the adjustments announced, one of the most significant concerned new language regarding the death penalty, specifying that Catholic tradition has allowed for use of the death penalty only when the identity and responsibility of the condemned is certain and capital punishment is the only way to protect the lives of others.

In keeping with *Evangelium Vitae*, the new edition, while not excluding capital punishment absolutely, limits its application to the following conditions: only in cases where the ultimate penalty of death is justified in order to secure the common good (but such cases today are very rare, if not practically nonexistent); there must be a full determination of the guilty party's responsibility and identity; the death penalty must be the only possible way of effectively defending human lives against the unjust aggressor; if nonlethal means are sufficient to defend and protect people's safety from the aggressor, authority will limit itself to such means.

"The Catholic tradition has allowed for use of the death penalty only when the identity . . . of the condemned is certain and capital punishment is the only way to protect the lives of others."

There is an important change in this latter condition: The original English text, which read "public authority should limit itself (to bloodless means)" was changed to "will limit itself to such means." Today, in fact, the state has the possibility for effectively preventing crime by rendering one who has committed an offense incapable of doing harm without definitively taking away from him the possibility of redeeming himself.

Following this line, on June 16, 1998, in the intervention which I made as head of the delegation of the Holy See to the conference held in Rome for the institution of an international criminal court, I was in a position to state:

"As an instrument of justice, such a court must be conceived as a means of seeking not revenge but the restoration of that right relationship within the human family which will lead to reconciliation. Accordingly, the verdicts, and most especially the sentences which the court will impose, must always keep in mind this higher goal of reconciliation. For that reason, the Holy See is convinced that the death penalty has no place in this statute. The destruction of life—be it as punishment or as panacea—is inconsistent with the universal norms that justify an international criminal court."

The Challenge Ahead

This leaves us, then, with the challenge to find a solution that punishes the convicted without violating his or her human dignity, while satisfying the need to protect public order and defend society. For Christians, our distaste for the death penalty is founded on our belief that every person has an inalienable right to life, because each human being is made in the image and likeness of God (Gn. 1:27). Such a challenge ought not be motivated by anger or fear, and must be more in line with the teachings of Christ's call to nonviolence.

We have seen that capital punishment is applied more for vengeance than for justice. We know that society's cry for it is more an impulsive "gut reaction," rather than one from the head. And we realize that just as pro-choice proponents wrongly try to draw a line when new life begins—at, for instance, three months, seven months or at birth—so too it is dangerous to draw a line when life can be extinguished.

In seeking a humane solution, we understand that forgiving the condemned is not the same as exonerating him or her from guilt and that capital punishment ultimately damages all of us by continuing the downward spiral of violence that is all too common in our society. Punishments, therefore, must be educative, not vindictive. "Punishment . . . has a medicinal purpose: As far as possible, it must contribute to the correction of the guilty party."

In closing, may I say that I believe that capital punishment, as the Holy Father said in St. Louis, is both "cruel and unnecessary." In essence, it is really a mask that covers the deeper issue we as a society are afraid to face: the lack of respect for human life—particularly of the preborn, the disabled and the elderly. Only when we have the courage to remove that mask will the sores hidden beneath it cease to fester. Only then will we—as individuals and as a society—begin the process of healing, moving away from a culture of death into a culture of life.

Capital Punishment Deserves Cautious Support

by James Nuechterlein

About the author: *James Nuechterlein is the editor of* First Things, *a monthly journal published by the Institute on Religion and Public Life.*

You get to a certain age and you know—or ought to know—what you think about important issues. Open-mindedness, when understood as a willingness to change one's mind if presented with new information or deeper insight, is a considerable virtue. But open-mindedness understood as perpetual indecision, a principled refusal to make up one's mind in the first place, is no virtue at all. It is evidence rather of intellectual and moral slack.

I have never had much trouble deciding what I think about things, or in being willing to share with others the views I hold. (Ask my wife and children.) But sometimes I waffle—and on no question more than capital punishment. I have come, after a lifetime of wrestling with the issue, to favor the death penalty. But I do so with unwonted uncertainty and uneasiness. The execution of Karla Faye Tucker in a Texas prison on February 3, 1998, brought out all my ambivalence.

Mixed Feelings Toward Capital Punishment

There was a time when I felt no ambivalence on capital punishment at all. I was firmly opposed. As editor of my college newspaper, I wrote an impassioned editorial condemning the execution of Caryl Chessman, a multiple murderer whose case roused national attention before his death in the San Quentin gas chamber in the spring of 1960. The death penalty, I argued, was a barbarism that no civilized society can countenance. Christians in particular, I added, should oppose capital punishment as a refusal to recognize life as God's sacred gift.

It was only over a long period of time that I came to change my mind. To be sure, many of the arguments against the death penalty have never impressed me. The suggestion, for example, that it is unconstitutional, a violation of the Eighth Amendment's prohibition of "cruel and unusual punishments," collapses in light of the fact that capital punishment is explicitly provided for elsewhere

Reprinted, with permission, from "An Unwonted Uncertainty," by James Nuechterlein, *First Things*, April 1998.

in the Constitution. Justice William Brennan's argument that "evolving moral standards" have changed the death penalty's constitutional standing was as blatant an expression of judicial imperialism as one could imagine: given the overwhelming approval of capital punishment by the American people and their elected representatives, Brennan could only mean that the robed guardians of the Court are sovereign arbiters not just of the constitutional text but of the moral principles that inform it. Acting in that sovereign capacity, they need be inhibited neither by the plain meaning of the text nor by the expressed will of the American people.

Other, more direct, arguments against the death penalty seem little more persuasive than the constitutional one. I have never quite understood, for instance, what people mean when they condemn capital punishment as an act of "vengeance." My dictionary defines "vengeance" as "punishment inflicted in retaliation for an injury or offense." In that sense, any form of punitive action against crime constitutes vengeance. Those who uphold the death penalty see it as an act of justice, not of revenge ("an act or instance of retaliating in order to get even").

There is among experts a good deal of debate as to whether the death penalty acts as a deterrent to prospective murderers. My dabbling in the technical literature leads me to the conclusion that the issue is unresolved (and perhaps, given the number and complexity of the variables involved, unresolvable). But even if it could be conclusively demonstrated that capital punishment has no deterrent effect, that would not clinch the case against it. Protection of society is one potential argument for executing murderers, but it is hardly the only, or even necessarily the decisive, one. Again, for most defenders of capital punishment, the primary issue is justice.

Some Christians, in the Catholic Church especially, have argued against the death penalty as part of a "consistent ethic of life." They include capital punishment in a package with such other issues as abortion and war. But that, it seems to me, muddies the moral waters. Christians should unequivocally oppose abortion because it takes innocent life. The difference with the death penalty, on this point at least, hardly requires argument. As to issues of war and peace, there is a venerable but by no means monolithic Christian tradition of pacifism. Most Christians—myself among them—think a more fruitful approach to the legitimacy of military action is to be found under the rubric of "just war." (Even most pacifists concede that World War II is a hard case for their position.) In any case, it would seem difficult to argue that opposition to war is morally of a piece, either in the Christian tradition or in Christian ethical analysis, with opposition to the death penalty.

> ***"Those who uphold the death penalty see it as an act of justice, not of revenge."***

But that is not to say there is no good case, Christian or otherwise, to be made against capital punishment. Moral philosophers have suggested that one test of the validity of the ethical positions we establish is their compatibility with our considered moral intuitions. For a great many people today, there are few if any such intuitions more compelling than the presumption, in all relevant situations, against the taking of life. (Thus the appeal to a "consistent ethic of life.") It is precisely that presumption that lies behind the argument I made as an undergraduate that the death penalty is inherently uncivilized, a moral atavism that diminishes respect for life and coarsens our moral sensibilities. Witness, in support of that argument, the unlovely spectacle of the drunken, cheering crowds that regularly materialize as an execution draws near. (Most defenders of the death penalty, of course, are as appalled by such spectacles as are those who oppose it.)

The dilemma for people like me is that in capital punishment we are confronted with competing moral intuitions. We acknowledge the presumption against the taking of life, but we also are possessed of a deep conviction that in certain circumstances the requirements of justice are most adequately met by imposition of the death sentence. Those who coldly and brutally take innocent life, we argue, may justly have their own lives taken in return. In so acting, society not only expresses its moral abhorrence of certain heinous crimes but also—paradoxically, but not, we think, contradictorily—indicates its reverence for innocent life.

It may well be that the case of Karla Faye Tucker confuses rather than clarifies the general argument about capital punishment. Hers was a special set of circumstances, which is why it attracted so much attention and brought to her side a number of people who normally favor the death penalty. I confess that, quite reflexively, I hoped her sentence would be commuted—although I'm not sure I could construct a rationally persuasive argument as to why, given the brutal double murder she participated in, hers should have been a case for leniency.

Perhaps it was simply that, in the almost fourteen years between her conviction and her execution, she had so transformed herself. Unlike most inhabitants of death row, she was attractive, winsome, and not given to self-pity or self-justification. She had undergone a manifestly genuine conversion to Christianity, and she faced the possibility of death with admirable courage and affecting faith. (Skeptics stressed the fact that she was white, but I saw no evidence that racial feelings played a significant role in garnering support for her.) None of that, of course, changed the fact of what she had done, and perhaps those who refused to lift her sentence were concerned most of all with the precedent they would thereby set. Hard cases, as they say, make bad law.

Still, my uncertainty about her execution remains, and though it does not change my mind on the death penalty in general, it reminds me that none of us who hold that position should ever feel entirely at ease with it or forget for a moment that we might be quite terribly wrong. And if we are wrong, the judgment for error on this life or death issue will weigh on us more severely than it will on those who, if it turns out that way, erred in the gentler direction.

Life Without Parole Is Preferable to the Death Penalty

by Bob Herbert

About the author: *Bob Herbert is a nationally syndicated columnist.*

Texas's bloodthirsty criminal justice officials have a dilemma. A Bible-quoting, Jesus-loving, reasonably normal looking woman named Karla Faye Tucker has been sentenced to death. Ordinarily the death penalty is no big deal in Texas, where liberals are required to carry visas and compassion is virtually illegal. It's a state that has shown itself perfectly willing to execute the retarded and railroad the innocent. But the scheduled execution of Ms. Tucker is another matter. Even in Texas, government officials are squeamish about zapping a woman.

As journalist Sam Howe Verhovek has noted in a *New York Times* article, Texas has not executed a woman since 1863, "when Chipita Rodriguez was put to death for murdering a horse trader."

Say hello to chivalry in a cowboy hat. Texas is by far the most backward state in the nation when it comes to capital punishment, but officials are searching high and low for a way to save the life of a woman who, before she got religion, joined with her boyfriend in taking a pickax to a sleeping couple, murdering them both.

According to Mr. Verhovek's story, Ms. Tucker "boasted, just after the killings, that she had experienced a surge of sexual pleasure every time she swung the 3-foot pickax."

But that's all in the past. Ms. Tucker is now seen as a good Christian woman, and Pat Robertson is among the many supporters of capital punishment who have come to her defense, urging that her life be spared.

There is hardly a better case to illustrate how capricious our approach to the death penalty is. Ms. Tucker's life may or may not be saved. But if some guy had committed a double murder and boasted that he got a sexual charge out of it, you wouldn't be able to find a so-called respectable public figure in all the United States who would go anywhere near the case.

As for Texas, the best thing about the Tucker case is the spotlight it is throwing on the state's fetish for capital punishment. Seventy-four people were executed in the U.S. in 1997, a modern record, and half of them were killed in Texas. One of those executed in Texas was David Wayne Spence. The biggest problem with his case was that he was almost certainly innocent.

> ***"Life without parole would . . . eliminate the grotesque danger that an innocent person will be put to death."***

The rest of the country actually experienced a decline in executions in 1997, according to the Death Penalty Information Center in Washington. Twenty-one states with the death penalty on the books had no executions in 1997. Even Georgia, once the death penalty capital of America, got through 1997 without executing anyone. No women were executed anywhere in the U.S. [Karla Faye Tucker was eventually executed on February 3, 1998.]

Opposition to the death penalty appears to be growing. Richard Dieter, director of the Information Center, which opposes capital punishment, noted that the American Bar Association and the Catholic Church are among a number of mainstream organizations that have criticized the arbitrary and inherently unfair ways in which the death penalty is applied.

In the fall of 1997, in Massachusetts, an attempt to reinstate the death penalty was defeated by one vote. A state representative who had planned to vote for reinstatement changed his mind after a jury convicted Louise Woodward, a 19-year-old British au pair, of murdering a child in her charge. The representative, John Slattery, disagreed with the verdict, which was later reduced by a judge to manslaughter.

Meanwhile, an increasing number of states that have the death penalty are passing laws making life without parole available as an alternative. When life without parole is an option, juries return fewer death penalty verdicts.

"I think this is sort of the wave of the future," said Mr. Dieter. "There will be greater use of life without parole as people gain confidence that it means what it says. I think what people want is safety. And they want punishment. Life without parole gives them that."

Life without parole addresses two of the most serious problems with the death penalty. It would be applied more equitably by judges and juries. The life or death crapshoot that passes for justice in capital cases would be eliminated. Life without parole would also eliminate the grotesque danger that an innocent person will be put to death.

It is interesting to note that in Texas life without parole is not available. Juries are thus forced to conclude that if they don't return a sentence of death, the murderer will someday be released.

The Death Penalty Is Preferable to Life Without Parole

by Wesley Lowe

About the author: *Wesley Lowe is a student at the Rochester Institute of Technology in Rochester, New York.*

Abolitionists claim that there are alternatives to the death penalty. They say that life in prison without parole serves just as well. Certainly, if you ignore all the murders criminals commit within prison when they kill prison guards and other inmates, and also when they kill decent citizens upon escape, like Dawud Mu'Min who was serving a 48-year sentence for the 1973 murder of a cab driver when he escaped a road work gang and stabbed to death a storekeeper named Gadys Nopwasky in a 1988 robbery that netted $4.00. Fortunately, there is now no chance of Mu'Min committing murder again. He was executed by the state of Virginia on November 14, 1997.

Another flaw is that life imprisonment tends to deteriorate with the passing of time. Take the Moore case in New York State for example.

In 1962, James Moore raped and strangled 14-year-old Pamela Moss. Her parents decided to spare Moore the death penalty on the condition that he be sentenced to life in prison without parole. Later on, thanks to a change in sentencing laws in 1982, James Moore is eligible for parole every two years!

If Pamela's parents knew that they couldn't trust the state, Moore could have been executed long ago and they could have put the whole horrible incident behind them forever. Instead they have a nightmare to deal with biannually. I'll bet not a day goes by that they don't kick themselves for being foolish enough to trust the liberal sham that is life imprisonment and rehabilitation. (According to the US Department of Justice, the average prison sentence served for murder is five years and eleven months.)

Reprinted, with permission, from "Capital Punishment vs. Life Without Parole," by Wesley Lowe, November 5, 1998, published on "Wesley Lowe's Pro–Death Penalty Web Page" at www.geocities.com/~lurch7/cp.html#life.

Putting a murderer away for life just isn't good enough. Laws change, so do parole boards, and people forget the past. Those are things that cause life imprisonment to wither away. As long as the murderer lives, there is always a chance, no matter how small, that he will strike again. And there are people who run the criminal justice system who are naive enough to allow him to repeat his crime.

Consider the case of Leroy Keith, a recidivist killer who became a major embarrassment to opponents of capital punishment. In 1934 Keith appeared at Warren, Ohio. There he walked up to a man named Frederick Griest as he was sitting behind the wheel of his parked car and shot him dead. Then he opened the car door, tumbled the slain man onto the pavement, and drove away in the vehicle. For that crime he was sentenced to death. An appeal resulted in a retrial. Again Keith was convicted and again he was sentenced to die. Another appeal resulted in the sentence being reduced to life imprisonment. On March 7, 1956, Keith was paroled. He was then given a government-mandated job in Youngstown, Ohio, with the Department of the County Engineer. He lasted there for three days before vanishing. On November 21, 1956, he turned up on North Howard Street in Akron, Ohio, where he walked up to a parked car and shot the driver, Coburn von Gunten, dead. He then dumped his body in the street and was about to drive off in his newly acquired car when nearby police officers intervened. Keith then engaged the police in a gun fight and managed to escape.

"For people who truly value public safety, there is no substitute for the best in its defense which is capital punishment."

Around the same time Keith also became the prime suspect in a grocery store robbery at Uniontown, Ohio, in which two people were shot to death.

When Ohio became too dangerous for him, Keith headed to New York City. He arrived in the Bronx and survived by robbing liquor stores and gas stations. On December 19, 1956, he joined three other men for the purpose of robbing a taxi. The foursome hailed a cab and were picked up by a driver named David Suro. When Keith pressed a gun to the back of Suro's head and demanded money, the man deliberately crashed his vehicle into a police car. The thieves jumped out of the disabled taxi and fled in different directions. Leroy Keith paused long enough to shoot the cab driver dead. Then he engaged police in a running gun battle through the crowded streets. Finally, five bullets brought him down. He survived his wounds and was charged with capital murder. He didn't get off with a prison sentence or parole this time. On July 23, 1959, his reign of terror ended when he was put to death by electrocution.

This is why for people who truly value public safety, there is no substitute for the best in its defense which is capital punishment. It not only forever bars the murderer from killing again, it also prevents parole boards and criminal rights activists from giving him the chance to repeat his crime.

Mentally Disadvantaged Killers Should Not Be Sentenced to Death

by Michael B. Ross

About the author: *Michael B. Ross has been on Connecticut's death row since June of 1987. Though currently under a stay of execution pending resolution of the appeals process, he expects to be executed before the year 2000.*

> The death penalty is an absolute punishment. If it is to be imposed at all, it should be imposed on people whose sense of responsibility and judgment is such that they fully appreciated the seriousness of what they were doing.

These words by David Bruck, a lawyer who has represented numerous capital defendants, appeared in the *International Herald Tribune* on June 23, 1987. Most people not only agree with the sentiment expressed but believe that only the most cunning and culpable of criminals are executed in this country—that the mentally ill and mentally retarded are explicitly excluded. Far too often, however, they are wrong.

As things now stand, mentally disadvantaged defendants often have to rely on a defense referred to as "diminished capacity." This simply means that such defendants may have known right from wrong but did not have full control over their actions, resulting in an inability to refrain from acts that people of average abilities could resist or simply would not commit.

The Problem with the "Diminished Capacity" Defense

Two basic problems face capital defendants trying to prove diminished capacity in court. The first is the skepticism with which most people view such a defense. All people are assumed to be normal and fully responsible for their actions, so it is the defendants' burden to prove otherwise.

Many people mistakenly believe that they can just look at a defendant and tell if he or she has a significant mental disorder. Even when a competent psychia-

Reprinted, with permission, from "Don't Execute Mentally Disturbed Killers," by Michael B. Ross, *The Humanist*, January/February 1999.

trist has diagnosed a mental illness or mental retardation, juries tend to dismiss the diagnosis if the defendant "looks normal."

There are several reasons for this. First, there is a general lack of confidence in psychiatric testimony. Second, there is a pervasive feeling that psychiatrists testifying for the defense will give whatever diagnosis is desired—and that psychiatrists testifying for the state are somehow more credible and less likely to be "bought." Third, it is generally assumed that a person whose life is on the line will feign a mental disorder and be able to fool even the best-trained psychiatrist. And finally, even if the defendant is proven to be mentally disturbed, it is often felt that she or he is somehow "getting away" with the crime. These feelings present formidable obstacles for any mentally disadvantaged defendant to overcome.

The second basic difficulty with proving diminished capacity has to do with the nature of capital crimes themselves. Often these are terrible crimes of a disturbing and heinous nature, and the trials can become extremely emotionally charged, leading many jurists to ignore even clear cases of a mental disorder.

The U.S. Supreme Court has mandated that mental disorders are mitigating factors, but this has not prevented mentally disadvantaged people from ending up on death row. It is estimated that 10 percent of all current death-row inmates are mentally ill and another 10 percent are mentally retarded. That translates to more than 600 mentally disadvantaged defendants currently under sentence of death in this country today. Some have already been executed.

Cases Involving Mentally Disadvantaged Defendants

Varnell Weeks was executed in Alabama for murder. Weeks had been diagnosed as being severely mentally ill and suffering from a "longstanding paranoid schizophrenia." Psychiatrists testifying for both the defense and prosecution agreed that he suffered from pervasive and bizarre religious delusions. Weeks believed that he was God, that his execution was part of a millennial religious scheme to destroy humankind, and that he would not die but, rather, would be transformed into a giant tortoise and reign over the universe.

An Alabama judge acknowledged that Weeks believed he was God in various manifestations and that he was a paranoid schizophrenic who suffered delusions. The judge's ruling went on to say that Weeks was "insane" according to "the dictionary generic definition of insanity" and what "the average person on the street would regard to be insane." However, the judge ruled that the electrocution could proceed because Weeks' ability to answer a few limited questions about his execution proved that he was legally "competent."

> ***"There is a general lack of confidence in psychiatric testimony."***

Morris Mason was executed in Virginia for murdering an elderly woman during an alcoholic rampage. She was burned to death after Mason had raped her, nailed her to a chair by the palms of her hands, and set the house on fire. Mason had a long history of mental illness and, prior to his arrest, had spent time in three state mental hospitals where he was diagnosed as mentally retarded and suffering from paranoid schizophrenia. In the week before the killing, he had twice sought help from his parole officer for his uncontrollable drinking and drug abuse. The day before the crime, he had asked to be placed in a halfway house but no openings were available.

"If the death penalty is to be maintained, it should clearly be limited to the most vicious, premeditated crimes. The acts of mentally disadvantaged criminals clearly do not qualify."

Johnny Frank Garrett was executed in Texas for the rape and murder of an elderly man. He was chronically psychotic and brain-damaged. One psychiatrist who examined Garrett described him as "one of the most psychiatrically impaired inmates" she had ever examined. Another said he had "one of the most virulent histories of abuse and neglect . . . encountered in over twenty-eight years of practice."

The late U.S. Supreme Court Justice Thurgood Marshall once wrote:

> At a time in our history when the streets of the nation's cities inspire fear and despair, rather than pride and hope, it is difficult to maintain objectivity and concern for our fellow citizens. But the measure of a country's greatness is its ability to retain compassion in times of crises.

If the death penalty is to be maintained, it should clearly be limited to the most vicious, premeditated crimes. The acts of mentally disadvantaged criminals clearly do not qualify. This distinction can be recognized by introducing verdicts of "guilty but mentally ill" and "guilty but mentally retarded," which would prohibit the death penalty in such cases and automatically impose sentences of life without the possibility of parole. This would offer some measure of protection to the mentally disadvantaged while guaranteeing the protection of the public. This is clearly the most logical and compassionate thing to do.

The Mental Competence of a Murderer Can Be Difficult to Determine

by Sam Howe Verhovek

About the author: *Sam Howe Verhovek is a staff writer for the* New York Times.

At a hearing in an Arkansas courtroom in April 1998, Charles Singleton basically argued for the right to make a choice: his sanity or his life.

Mr. Singleton, 39, on death row for the 1979 murder of a grocer named Mary Lou York, is on anti-schizophrenia medication, which, the state argues, makes him mentally competent enough to be executed. But Mr. Singleton wants to stop taking the drugs, which could well make him sufficiently delusional that state psychologists would not certify him as ready to be put to death.

"We have to convince the court that you can't involuntarily medicate to competency if that is what is making him executable," explains Mr. Singleton's lawyer, Jeff Rosenzweig.

The Larger Debate

While Mr. Singleton's case is a particularly complex legal matter, it is also part of a much broader debate hashed out in courtrooms across the nation: when is a convicted murderer so mentally deficient that he or she earns the right to be spared execution?

The question is not so much whether society should execute people who are insane, since the United States Supreme Court has firmly ruled, and even staunch death penalty proponents generally say they agree, that people who are truly mentally incompetent should not be put to death. Rather, it is how competence should be determined.

Many supporters of capital punishment insist that the number of death-row inmates who are so mentally impaired that they should not be executed is exceedingly small. And they are clearly unimpressed with Mr. Singleton's arguments, and similar ones being made by at least two condemned men in Texas.

"They're sane enough to know that by stopping their medication, they will not be executed," said Dudley Sharp, vice president of Justice for All, a Texas-based victims' rights group that strongly supports the death penalty. "Is that the reasoning of a sane man or an insane man? It sounds very sane to me."

The legal dockets are full of cases in which lawyers for the condemned argue that their clients aren't fit to die; most such appeals get tossed out, in large part because the jury that sentenced the prisoner to death determined that he or she was not insane, at least at the time of the murder. But what about cases in which a murderer's mental health declines after his sentencing?

"When is a convicted murderer so mentally deficient that he or she earns the right to be spared execution?"

That is the primary issue in an extremely unusual hearing now under way in California involving 39-year-old Horace Kelly, a man who often sits in his own waste in his cell and who says he believes that death row is a vocational school. Mr. Kelly was sentenced to death years ago for fatally shooting two women and an 11-year-old boy in 1984. Now, though, a new 12-member jury is being convened to decide whether Mr. Kelly has become too incompetent since the time of his sentencing to be executed.

If the jury rules that Mr. Kelly is incompetent, thus sparing his life, at least for the time being, state officials want to send him to a prison mental hospital for treatment. They hope in such a circumstance to improve his condition enough to execute him, a policy that the American Medical Association opposes.

And, in another twist, some lawyers in capital cases have seized on statements by their clients who say they wish to die: Isn't that sentiment itself a sign of incompetence? Take the case of Wilford Lee Berry Jr., an Ohio death-row inmate who has been called "The Volunteer" because of his stated wish that he be put to death as sentenced, and thus become the first person executed in that state in 35 years.

Political Decisions

In April 1998, a Federal judge continued a stay of the execution pending a competency hearing for Mr. Berry, 35, who was convicted of killing his boss, a Cleveland baker, in 1989. Citing in part his stated wish to die, Mr. Berry's mother and sister have petitioned to file a challenge to his death sentence.

Two state-certified psychiatrists have said that although Mr. Berry suffers from several personality disorders, he is competent to be executed, while a third psychologist who examined him said he was incompetent.

Another case involves Gary Heidnik, a Pennsylvania death-row inmate convicted in a horrendous case of torture-murder in the basement of his home, in which he cut up the body of one of his female captives with an electric saw, cooked her head and fed her flesh to another captive. He has been diagnosed as a paranoid schizophrenic, and his execution has been repeatedly put off pending a ruling on his mental status.

In 1986, the Supreme Court, in a 5–4 decision, ruled that executing the mentally incompetent violated the Constitution's ban on cruel and unusual punishment. Richard C. Dieter, executive director of the Death Penalty Information Center, a group that opposes capital punishment, said the standard was a sound moral one.

"There is no message of justice sent to just inflict pointless punishment on someone who doesn't know what's happening," he said.

But Mr. Dieter and other advocates argue that with decisions on competence generally left up to judges and Governors who believe themselves to be under enormous public pressure to enforce the death penalty, there are many cases in which people who are not competent are put to death.

In one of the most controversial cases involving questions of competence, then-Gov. Bill Clinton of Arkansas left the Presidential campaign trail in 1992 to fly home for the execution of Rickey Ray Rector, a murderer who had blown away part of his brain in a suicide attempt just after he shot and killed a police officer. Mr. Rector was so brain-damaged, his lawyers said, that he asked that his dessert of pecan pie be put aside for him to eat as a snack after his execution. Mr. Clinton rejected his final clemency appeal.

> ***"Some lawyers in capital cases have seized on statements by their clients who say they wish to die: Isn't that sentiment itself a sign of incompetence?"***

The question of competency is, of course, hardly the only one involving a judgment on the state of mind of a killer.

The controversy that raged earlier in 1998 over Texas's execution of Karla Faye Tucker went to the heart of the question of whether a killer can be so rehabilitated on death row that he or she earns the right to be spared execution.

Last Resorts

In yet one more legal tangle surrounding the question of fitness to face the death penalty, some condemned inmates have sought another way out.

They have attempted to injure themselves just before their executions, thus putting themselves in the hospital and, perhaps, securing a doctor's opinion that they are not well enough to be wheeled onto the death chamber gurney.

In 1997 in Texas, 39-year-old David Lee Herman managed to break apart a prison-issue razor and slash his throat and wrist two days before his execution. He was so cut up that he was sent to an infirmary, but there, state doctors managed to stitch him up so he could be put to death as scheduled.

Bibliography

Books

Mumia Abu-Jamal — *Live from Death Row*. Reading, MA: Addison-Wesley, 1995.

James R. Acker, Robert M. Bohm, and Charles S. Lanier, eds. — *America's Experiment With Capital Punishment: Reflections on the Past, Present, and Future of the Ultimate Penal Sanction*. Durham, NC: Carolina Academic Press, 1998.

Jan Arriens, ed. — *Welcome to Hell: Letters and Writings from Death Row*. Boston: Northeastern University Press, 1997.

Hugo Adam Bedau — *The Death Penalty in America: Current Controversies*. 4th ed. New York: Oxford University Press, 1997.

Walter Berns — *For Capital Punishment: Crime and the Morality of the Death Penalty*. Lanham, MD: University Press of America, 1991.

Mark Costanzo — *Just Revenge: Costs and Consequences of the Death Penalty*. New York: St. Martin's, 1997.

Gardner C. Hanks — *Against the Death Penalty: Christian and Secular Arguments Against Capital Punishment*. Scottsdale, PA: Herald, 1997.

Jesse Jackson — *Legal Lynching: Racism, Injustice, and the Death Penalty*. New York: Marlowe, 1996.

Robert Johnson — *Death Work: A Study of the Modern Execution Process*. Belmont, CA: Wadsworth, 1997.

James J. Megivern — *The Death Penalty: An Historical and Theological Survey*. Mahwah, NJ: Paulist Press, 1997.

Michael A. Mello and David Von Drehle — *Dead Wrong: A Death Row Lawyer Speaks Out Against Capital Punishment*. Madison: University of Wisconsin Press, 1998.

Debbie Morris — *Forgiving the Dead Man Walking*. Grand Rapids, MI: Zondervan, 1998.

Louis P. Pojman and Jeffrey Reiman — *The Death Penalty: For and Against*. New York: Rowman and Littlefield, 1998.

Helen Prejean — *Dead Man Walking: An Eyewitness Account of the Death Penalty in the United States*. New York: Random House, 1993.

Mei Ling Rein, Nancy R. Jacobs, and Mark A. Siegel, eds. — *Capital Punishment: Cruel and Unusual?* Wylie, TX: Information Plus, 1998.

Bryan Vila and Cynthia Morris, eds. — *Capital Punishment in the United States*. Westport, CT: Greenwood, 1997.

Robert V. Wolf and Austin Sarat, eds. — *Capital Punishment: Crime, Justice, and Punishment.* Broomall, PA: Chelsea House, 1997.

Periodicals

Hadley Arkes — "My Evening with Jesse," *Crisis*, June 1997. Available from PO Box 10559, Riverton, NJ 08076-0559.

Walter Berns and Joseph Bessette — "Why the Death Penalty Is Fair," *Wall Street Journal*, January 9, 1998.

Shannon Brownlee et al. — "The Place for Vengeance," *U.S. News & World Report*, June 16, 1997.

William F. Buckley Jr. — "Miss Tucker's Plea," *National Review*, March 9, 1998.

Fox Butterfield — "Behind the Death Row Bottleneck," *New York Times*, December 25, 1998.

John J. DiIulio — "Abolish the Death Penalty, Officially," *Wall Street Journal*, December 15, 1997.

Economist — "The Death Penalty: One in Seven Wasn't Guilty," November 28, 1998.

Lawrence D. Egbert — "Physicians and the Death Penalty," *America*, March 7, 1998.

Christopher John Farley and James Willwerth — "Dead Teen Walking," *Time*, January 19, 1998.

Samuel Francis — "Death Row Reflects Reality, Not Discrimination," *Conservative Chronicle*, February 11, 1998. Available from Box 29, Hampton, IA 50441.

Eric M. Freedman — "The Case Against the Death Penalty," *USA Today*, March 1, 1997.

Jonathan Gromer — "Machines of Death," *Popular Mechanics*, January 1, 1998.

Bob Herbert — "Mistakes Were Made," *New York Times*, January 11, 1998.

Michael Higgins — "Is Capital Punishment for Killers Only?" *ABA Journal*, August 1997.

Jet — "Study Cites Link Between Death Penalty and Race," June 22, 1998.

David A. Kaplan — "Life and Death Decisions," *Newsweek*, June 16, 1997.

John Kavanaugh — "Killing Persons, Killing Ethics," *America*, July 19, 1997.

Sara Kelly — "Innocence by Association," *Mother Jones*, March 1, 1999.

David L. Kirp — "Death Watch," *Dissent*, Fall 1996.

Bibliography

Charles Lane	"Lethal Objection," *New Republic*, March 2, 1998.
John McCormick	"The Wrongly Condemned," *Newsweek*, November 9, 1998.
Edmund F. McGarrell and Marla Sandys	"The Misperception of Public Opinion Toward Capital Punishment," *American Behavioral Scientist*, February 1996.
Patricia Pearson	"Sex Discrimination on Death Row," *New York Times*, January 13, 1998.
Fred Pelka	"Unequal Justice: Preserving the Rights of the Mentally Retarded in the Criminal Justice System," *Humanist*, November 21, 1997.
Michael B. Ross	"The Execution of Innocence," *Peace Review*, September 1998.
Joseph P. Shapiro	"The Wrong Men on Death Row," *U.S. News & World Report*, November 9, 1998.
Suzanne D. Strater	"The Juvenile Death Penalty: In the Best Interests of the Child?" *Human Rights*, Spring 1995. Available from the ABA Press for the Section of Individual Rights and Responsibilities of the American Bar Association, 750 N. Lake Shore Dr., Chicago, IL 60611.
Andrew Peyton Thomas	"Penalty Box: A Much-Needed Reform Seemed Poised to Hasten Executions—Until Federal Judges Got Their Hands on It," *National Review*, May 4, 1998.

Organizations to Contact

The editors have compiled the following list of organizations concerned with the issues debated in this book. The descriptions are derived from materials provided by the organizations. All have publications or information available for interested readers. The list was compiled on the date of publication of the present volume; the information provided here may change. Be aware that many organizations take several weeks or longer to respond to inquiries, so allow as much time as possible.

American Civil Liberties Union (ACLU)
Capital Punishment Project
125 Broad St., 18th Fl., New York, NY 10004
(212) 549-2500 • fax: (212) 549-2646
website: http://www.aclu.org

The project is dedicated to abolishing the death penalty. The ACLU believes that capital punishment violates the Constitution's ban on cruel and unusual punishment as well as the requirements of due process and equal protection under the law. It publishes and distributes numerous books and pamphlets, including *The Case Against the Death Penalty* and *Frequently Asked Questions Concerning the Writ of Habeas Corpus and the Death Penalty.*

Amnesty International USA (AI)
322 Eighth Ave., New York, NY 10001
(212) 807-8400 • fax: (212) 627-1451
website: http://www.amnesty-usa.org

Amnesty International is an independent worldwide movement working impartially for the release of all prisoners of conscience, fair and prompt trials for political prisoners, and an end to torture and executions. AI is funded by donations from its members and supporters throughout the world. AI has published several books and reports, including *Fatal Flaws: Innocence and the Death Penalty.*

Canadian Coalition Against the Death Penalty (CCADP)
PO Box 38104, 550 Eglinton Ave. W, Toronto, ON M5N 3A8 CANADA
(416) 693-9112 • fax: (416) 686-1630
e-mail: ccadp@home.com • website: http://www.ccadp.org

CCADP is a not-for-profit international human rights organization dedicated to educating the public on alternatives to the death penalty worldwide and to providing emotional and practical support to death row inmates, their families, and the families of murder victims. The coalition releases pamphlets and periodic press releases, and its website includes a student resource center providing research information on capital punishment.

Death Penalty Focus of California
74 New Montgomery, Suite 250, San Francisco, CA 94105
(415) 243-0143 • fax: (415) 243-0994
e-mail: info@deathpenalty.org • website: http://www.deathpenalty.org

Death Penalty Focus of California is a nonprofit organization dedicated to the abolition of capital punishment through grassroots organization, research, and the dissemination of information about the death penalty and its alternatives. It publishes the quarterly newsletter *The Sentry*.

Death Penalty Information Center (DPIC)
1606 20th St. NW, 2nd Fl., Washington, DC 20009
(202) 347-2531
website: http://www.essential.org/dpic

DPIC conducts research into public opinion on the death penalty. The center believes capital punishment is discriminatory and excessively costly and that it may result in the execution of innocent persons. It publishes numerous reports, such as *Millions Misspent: What Politicians Don't Say About the High Costs of the Death Penalty*, *Innocence and the Death Penalty: Assessing the Danger of Mistaken Executions*, and *With Justice for Few: The Growing Crisis in Death Penalty Representation*.

Justice Fellowship (JF)
PO Box 16069, Washington, DC 20041-6069
(703) 904-7312 • fax: (703) 478-9679
website: http://www.justicefellowship.org

This Christian organization bases its work for reform of the justice system on the concept of victim-offender reconciliation. It does not take a position on the death penalty, but it publishes the pamphlet *Capital Punishment: A Call to Dialogue*.

Justice for All (JFA)
PO Box 55159, Houston, TX 77255
(713) 935-9300 • fax: (713) 935-9301
e-mail: jfanet@msn.com • website: http://www.jfa.net

Justice for All is a not-for-profit criminal justice reform organization that supports the death penalty. Its activities include circulating online petitions to keep violent offenders from being paroled early and publishing the monthly newsletter *The Voice of Justice*.

Justice Now
PO Box 62132, North Charleston, SC 29419-2132
e-mail: ranlerch@geocities.com • website: http://www.geocities.com/CapitolHill/8169

This organization supports the death penalty as a solution to the problems of crime and overcrowded prisons in the United States. It maintains information resources, which are available to the public, consisting of books, pamphlets, periodicals, newspaper clippings, and bibliographies about serial killers, death row prisoners, executions, prisons, and courts.

Lamp of Hope Project
PO Box 305, League City, TX 77574-0305
e-mail: ksebung@c-com.net • website: http://www.lampofhope.org

The project was established and is run primarily by Texas death row inmates. It works for victim-offender reconciliation and for the protection of the civil rights of prisoners, particularly the right of habeas corpus appeal. It publishes and distributes the periodic *Texas Death Row Journal*.

Lincoln Institute for Research and Education
1001 Connecticut Ave. NW, Washington, DC 20036
(202) 223-5112

The institute is a conservative think tank that studies public policy issues affecting the lives of black Americans, including the issue of the death penalty, which it favors. It publishes the quarterly *Lincoln Review.*

National Coalition to Abolish the Death Penalty (NCADP)
1436 U St. NW, Suite 104, Washington, DC 20009
(202) 387-3890 • fax: (202) 387-5590
e-mail: info@ncadp • website: http://www.ncadp.org

The National Coalition to Abolish the Death Penalty is a collection of more than 115 groups working together to stop executions in the United States. The organization compiles statistics on the death penalty. To further its goal, the coalition publishes *Legislative Action to Abolish the Death Penalty*, information packets, pamphlets, and research materials.

National Criminal Justice Reference Service (NCJRS)
U.S. Department of Justice
PO Box 6000, Rockville, MD 20849-6000
(301) 519-5500 • (800) 851-3420
e-mail: askncjrs@ncjrs.org • website: http://www.ncjrs.org

The National Criminal Justice Reference Service is one of the most extensive sources of information on criminal and juvenile justice in the world. For a nominal fee, this clearinghouse provides topical searches and reading lists on many areas of criminal justice, including the death penalty. It publishes an annual report on capital punishment.

Index

Index